How to Get Your Child off the Refrigerator and on to Learning

Homeschooling Highly Distractible, ADHD, or Just Plain Fidgety Kids

Carol Barnier

Emerald
Books
P.O. Box 635
Lynnwood, WA 98046

D1411305

Emerald Books are distributed through YWAM Publishing. For a full list of titles, including other home-schooling resources, visit our website at www.ywampublishing.com or call 1-800-922-2143.

**How to Get Your Child off the Refrigerator and on to Learning:
Homeschooling Highly Distractible, ADHD, or Just Plain Fidgety Kids**

10 09 08 07 06 05 04 03 /   10 9 8 7 6 5 4 3 2

Published by Emerald Books
P.O. Box 635
Lynnwood, Washington 98046

ISBN: 1-883002-70-2

Printed in the United States of America.

Contents

Acknowledgments

Special thanks are due to a number of people for their contributions to this book:

To my son Glenn, who provided all the inspiration for this book.

To my loving husband, who believed in this book long before I'd ever written the first word.

To friends who helped with feedback, kinds words, and child care; one most especially whose editing advice was priceless. Danke.

Put the Label on the Table

You're going to notice in this book that I do not shy away from putting a label on my child. This is an issue that many parents struggle with. In reading this book, you will conclude that I am of the philosophy that a label is not to be feared, for it brings empowerment. I certainly understand when many parents express concern that their child will receive a label and choose to hang their self-image upon the deficits that it proclaims. While I know this is a possibility and have even seen it happen, it is easily preventable. I believe that having a label brings so many positives to the equation that it is almost essential for real progress. Let me explain.

I am five feet tall and absolutely zero inches, but only if you measure me early in the morning and squint while doing so. Now, you can pretend I'm not short. You can avoid using the "s" word around me throughout my entire childhood. What if I thought I was as tall as everyone else? What if I thought I should be able to reach the top kitchen shelves as easily as my taller peers? Imagine my frustration if I believed you. What if I began to think that I must be lazy or stupid or that something else even more mysterious was wrong with me because I couldn't do as easily what others could? You may think this is a weak analogy because my abbreviated height would be so evident that I couldn't possibly miss it. But I would contend that my son couldn't possibly miss that his behavior and struggles with focus were blatantly different from other children. To pretend that there was "nothing wrong" or nothing different when it was so obvious to him that things were quite different would create confusion in his mind. Naturally, he will search for answers that would explain the clear differences. And what conclusions do kids usually come up with? "I'm a bad kid." "I'm weird." "I'm stupid."

> **The first thing a label does is give a concrete name to the jumbled issues that have been a constant part of this child's life.**

The first thing a label does is give a concrete name to the jumbled issues that have been a constant part of this child's life. It doesn't convey a judgment of good or bad, it simply says, "We know what this is." This usually brings great relief; it says, "We're not crazy. There is something going on here." If there's a problem with labeling, it comes when we allow our children to define themselves by this label. We as parents *cannot* allow this to happen.

Let's go back to the analogy of my height. Because I am now permitted this label of "short," I finally understand why I've been having trouble in areas where others have not. I wasn't stupid or lazy after all. I was short! However, does this now relieve me from the responsibility of putting away items that go on the top shelves? Does this mean I don't have to try to sink a basketball in my P.E. class? Does it mean I don't have to hang up my clothes because the reach is much more of a stretch for me than for others? *Of course not!* I have to find other strategies to work around my stature, but it in *no way* alleviates my responsibility to get the tasks done. If I allow my child to be exempt from his responsibilities in this world because it is more difficult for him, I have done him great harm. The label is not a vehicle that excuses us from any responsibility. It simply explains why some things are harder.

Another disadvantage of giving a label is that some children might take this as an opportunity to feel sorry for themselves. They may accept that the label names their obvious condition. They might even reluctantly accept that they must still achieve. But they will whine and carry a bucket of misery about the house as they must go through life with this incredible burden. *Don't buy it!* And don't let them buy it. If you feel sorry for your child and allow them a deficient set of expectations, you are more damaging than twenty labels. All of us have a set of conditions that limit us in one way or another. All of us have obstacles to overcome. But having difficulty in focusing in no way exempts one from achievement. Don't let your child focus on a disability. In fact, disability is not really a good word. Different abilities would be more appropriate. In our house, I have made sure that my son is well-acquainted with people whose challenges far surpass his own. Have your children read about Joni Eareckson Tada, or Heather Whitestone, our first deaf Miss America. Have them read about Helen Keller, who conquered insurmountable challenges. My son doesn't have to achieve a life that is impossible, but he *is* expected to achieve all that is possible for him. Though it isn't easy, achievement is still the expectation, and the paths to achieving the possible may be different for each child.

Is This Book About My Child?

Which child is yours? The super-wiggly? The highly charged? The inattentive? The energetic? The impulsive? The daydreamer? The spirited? The distractible? The unbridled, intense, passionate child? Or all of them? No matter how you define the qualities in your special child, the common thread is how difficult it is to keep some children focused on a task until they complete it. And schoolwork is an unending line of tasks waiting for completion. If you are reading this book, chances are you know all too well what I'm talking about. This book is for anyone who teaches one of these challenging, highly distractible children.

I sought solutions to the problems presented by just such a child. In our situation we had a clear case of an ADHD (Attention-Deficit/Hyperactivity Disorder) diagnosis. Over time we developed techniques that proved highly successful with our child. But we soon came to learn that the ideas work well with any child who struggles with focus. So while the exact diagnosis for your child may be different or significantly lesser in degree, the techniques suggested here will work just as well. In fact, they are used in our house just as often with my calm, highly focused and disciplined daughter. She just thinks they're fun. So while you may hear a "bent" in the language of this book toward ADHD children because of our personal experiences, keep in mind your own child and how he or she would respond to these educational solutions. And start enjoying your school day.

You CAN Teach This Child!

The verdict was in. My son was a clear-cut case of an ADHD (Attention-Deficit/Hyperactivity Disorder) child. The kindergarten teacher agreed. The doctor agreed. The psychologist agreed. Frankly, I agreed. But now, what do we do? I had six weeks until my son would start first grade, and the only solution being suggested was Ritalin. Feeling we didn't have enough time to make an informed decision about the long-term use of this very powerful drug, we began to homeschool...but only to buy us time. We had no expectation that we would continue this forever. (God knew I wasn't ready for the big picture yet.) And yet as time went on, it became very clear to us that our home was the best environment in which my son could learn. Indeed, it was the only environment in which he could thrive. And thrive he did...eventually.

I would love to say that it was a breeze from the moment I rang that first school bell. (No kidding. I actually did this.) But we were in for a major adjustment. You see, like many moms new to homeschooling, I attempted to emulate the current methods used in public schools when designing our homeschool program. BIG MISTAKE. An especially big mistake with a focus-challenged child. But no one told me that. I sought out the advice of those with sweet, quiet, compliant children and then tried to impose it on my own spirited child. It didn't work. It couldn't work. But no one told me that either. I found volumes of information on how to recognize ADHD children, how to manage them, how to medicate them, how to discipline them, and how to accept them. I attended seminars and read books about the ADHD child, only to discover for the umpteenth time that it could be diet, it could be behavioral, it could be TV, etc. And while I certainly was interested in all the "what-it-could-be's," I still needed to know how to teach math tomorrow. And no one told me that.

So after six pretty awful months of trials and errors, of tears and tantrums (mine as well as his), and of working to establish that I was, indeed, the boss, we began to find our groove. Slowly, our daily routine began to improve. After I let go of any preconceived notions of how he *should* learn, I just experimented till we found how he did learn. We haven't looked back since. And homeschooling has become the blessing in our lives that it should be.

The hallmark of ADHD children is that they constantly change from one day to the next. Inconsistency will be your constant companion.

You can teach your highly distractible child. You can even do it with a two-year-old tying your shoe laces together. There are tricks and methods that will put joy into the learning experience and will take the frustration out of your day. The purpose of this book is to share some of the ideas that we and others have used successfully in homeschooling our challenging children.

Some of the things you will learn are:

- How to help your child focus when there are four other kids in the room.
- A phonics program where every lesson is a quick game that kids love.
- How to see ADHD as a gift to be explored, not a burden to be overcome.
- How to make even a math workbook fun.
- How to deal with a child constantly in motion.
- Why 3 x 5 cards are a homeschooler's best tool.
- How to choose the environment in which this spirited child can best learn.

The hallmark of ADHD children is that they constantly change from one day to the next. Inconsistency will be your constant companion. The approach that worked so well all of last week suddenly seems to have hit a brick wall this week. Because your child is unique every day, you are always in unchartered waters. You do not have the luxury of being able to implement the work or ideas of others. Your task is not cut and dried. You must see yourself as a scientist/inventor/explorer—more like George Washington Carver or Thomas Edison—constantly trying new ideas until you hit upon those that work with your child. So, starting now, let go of your preconceived ideas about what your homeschool should look like. Take on an experimental attitude. Follow your instincts. Pick and use only those ideas from this book that you feel would work for your child. Experiment with them. Adjust them. Mold them. If they don't work, pitch them. The goal here is learning.

Chapter 1

Life with the Spirited Child

Yes, I really found him on top of the refrigerator. Fortunately, he accepted my one constructive criticism of this event, and it hasn't been repeated. But many times I have turned the corner to find my son swinging from the doorjams. While most people are aware that ADHD children possess great volumes of energy and an inability to focus, only those of us who live with them have come to know and love that delightful quality known as "Impulse Control." Couple these characteristics with a lack of fear for personal safety and a much greater emphasis on their own feelings rather than the feelings of others, and you have the general recipe for an ADHD kid. You also have the recipe for trouble in your schooling day—not to mention life in general.

However, the positive side to this is that these qualities make for a life full of wonderful surprises and filled with heaps of laughter. Or at least it can be. But that is primarily up to you, the parent/teacher. Case in point. Just when I think my son can't do anything new to surprise me…he does. One night about a year ago, he came rushing into my room, out of breath, to inform me that something "really serious" had happened. It somehow involved flying pieces of broken light bulb glass and smoke. Fearing an impending fire, I flew to the site of concern. Sure enough, there was a light bulb with a substantial portion missing.

I found the offending piece lying almost ten feet from the lamp. I wondered at the laws of physics that had been at work when I saw what looked like the remnants of a waterdrop on the piece of glass. I asked my son if water had been dropped onto the bulb. With very deliberate speech, he said that perhaps when he had been talking a piece of saliva had been expelled onto the bulb. Why had he been talking to a lamp?, I thought. Then I noticed the desert dry rivulets of previous spit streams that were encrusted upon this defenseless bulb. "Glenn...?" I called quietly to my son. I was using an incredulous tone that said "What I'm thinking might have happened here couldn't really have happened." "Glenn," I said again, "have you actually been spitting on this light bulb?" No answer. He gave me a very wide-eyed, fearful expression. Let's try again. "Glenn, why were you spitting on this light bulb?" I could visualize seventeen or eighteen wheels turning in his head. Finally, the answer I shall never forget emerged. "Because I liked the sizzle." In spite of the clear dangers, I burst out laughing.

> **ADHD children do indeed like the sizzle. They like to see the sizzle, hear the sizzle, and often be the sizzle.**

I know many children go through a saying "No!" stage. Some go through a "biting" stage. But no one ever warned me about the "spitting-on-light bulbs" stage. Well, after a long talk about the obvious dangers, I think the other light bulbs in the house are now safe. If he starts looking curiously at the electrical outlets, who knows where we'll end up?

I think the most revealing part of that story can be summed up in the line "I like the sizzle!" ADHD children do indeed like the sizzle. They like to see the sizzle, hear the sizzle, and often be the sizzle. This is a part of their wonderfulness. It is also a part of what can be most difficult about raising and educating them. How they perceive that "sizzle" in themselves is up to you.

This Child IS Different

You must grow comfortable with the fact that this child is different. Others may not see it. You cannot depend upon their assessment of your child. They will try to convince you that it is a discipline problem or that there must be "trouble" at home or that you should eliminate wallpaper paste from their diet, etc. But I have learned time and time again that what works for most children often has little bearing on what will work with my child.

I remember a time when my son was having minor separation problems when I would drop him off at a church function. I took to heart a tip I learned at a recent MOPS (Mothers of Preschoolers) meeting and attempted the "Tissue-Kiss." That's where you kiss a tissue while wearing lipstick and the remaining imprint is folded and given to your child. Then, when they are in day care or any place without you, they can pull out the kiss if they are missing you and *voila!* Instant reassurance. What a wonderful idea, I thought. It fills me with the warm fuzzies just thinking about it.

I kissed the tissue, handed it to him, and explained that he could have this as a kiss from me whenever he felt he needed one.

Well, here's how it played out in our house. My two children and I were on our way to this aforementioned church meeting. I decided to use this reaffirming "tissue-kiss" for my son, just to let him know I loved him. I kissed the tissue, handed it to him, and explained that he could have this as a kiss from me whenever he felt he needed one while I was away at the meetings. I smiled over at him, expecting that warm and fuzzy expression to break out all over his face. He looked puzzled, but made no comment. After a few moments he asked me for a kiss. As my lips still held a fair amount of lipstick, I declined, saying I didn't want to dirty up his face. He kind of smiled and then pursued the issue again. He wanted a kiss. I was certain by this time that he just wanted me to mess his face up...in keeping with his love of drawing on himself with magic markers, showing me the chewed-up contents of his mouth—you know the drill. So again, I declined the kiss.

We rode on in silence for several minutes. But soon the silence was broken by the saddest cry and the biggest tear-filled eyes I had ever seen. "What's wrong?" I pleaded. I could scarcely understand him through his tears, but finally I determined that he thought I had decided that he would be getting no more "real" kisses, and that from now on, all kisses would be received from a tissue. He was telling me that I loved lipstick more than I loved him and that we should throw out all lipsticks, and that mommies should give their kids real kisses...and so on and so on.

Well you've never seen lipstick come off so fast in your life. At the next stoplight, I plastered that boy's face with as many kisses as it could hold with several tickles on the side. When he said through his laughter, "The light's green!" I defiantly answered, "I don't care!" and kept on kissing him. (There wasn't traffic behind me.)

So if you've ever thought that perhaps what works for most children may not work for each child, remember my son. What a wondrous gift I received in learning just how important a mother's touch is to a happy child. I won't forget again.

Finding What Works for YOUR Child

It took a great deal of time for me to get to the point where I trusted my God-given instincts and love for this child over the advice of others. Every time one of these "others" would present a solution theory or even implied one to me, I agonized over it. I researched

Keep searching until
you find the right key!

this new "root" cause of our problem, rearranged my teaching and discipline efforts and eventually, exhausted, I collapsed again into despair, because my child had NOT turned into the picture that I saw in so many other children.

Finally, in desperation and perhaps even in defeat, I gave up trying to make him like other children and decided that we would have to let him learn what he can in whatever way he can. I lowered my expectations. I carried the wrong assumption that if he cannot learn as other children do, then this probably means that he cannot learn, at least not as much as I was hoping. So I dumped the usual methods of learning and tried different methods to see what worked best with him. Then, amazingly, "it" began to happen. When I experimented and found what worked for him, not only did he learn, he flourished.

> **I gave up trying to make him like other children and decided that we would have to let him learn what he can in whatever way he can.**

When it comes to highly distractible children, we don't need to lower our expectations. We just need to accept that they need other methods of meeting them. In fact, we need to raise our expectations. We need to provide activity, challenge, and discipline that match their level of energy and capability. We need to believe and share with our children the belief that God made them this way for a reason. There are amazing achievements they will be able to accomplish that the rest of us in this world wouldn't have the energy for. It is our job and privilege to find that glorious outcome for this special child.

Your Job Is to Find the Right Key

Take responsibility for when your child does not learn. In our school we have the concept of "The Keys." This makes clear to the student and the teacher exactly what their responsibilities are regarding the learning process. I believe that every item to be learned can be learned in more than one way. There are several "keys" to unlock understanding of any piece of information. If I present something to my son and he does not get it, I have given him the wrong key! It is not his job to take this key and jam it into the lock of his brain and try to make it fit—even if it fits for ninety-nine other kids 99% of the time. If it's the wrong key for him, it's the wrong key. It *is* his job, though, to tell me that I've given the wrong key. He is not allowed to nod his head and pretend he understands when he doesn't. Now, instead of feeling defeated and stupid, the child can now be proactive in finding a solution. He no longer has to say, "Sorry, Mommy, I still don't get it. I'm sorry my brain doesn't work like it should." Instead, he can say, "That key didn't work. I guess you need to find another one." It takes the burden off of the child when he doesn't understand something and puts it squarely back on the teacher, where I believe it belongs. I don't intend for this to overwhelm you. All of us need to be liberated from the idea that if it works for other kids it must work for ours. I simply want you to free yourself from thinking in a box. Step outside the box. Keep searching until you find the exact key that will unlock the information for your child.

Accept Your Child's Inability to Focus

Next, stop expecting that today will be the day that your child learns to focus. I used to become so angry at the amount of time my son wasted in allowing his mind to wander. I was sure that it was purposeful on his part. I knew that if he just tried, he could focus. One day, though, I realized that he was trying. He was *really* trying. And to his own frustration, still, his mind wandered. That's when I added another item to my list of responsibilities. It is my job to bring his attention back to his work. At least for this time of his life, this is my job. About every fourth sentence out of my mouth in our school day is "Eyes back on your work" or "Let's focus" or "Pencil to the paper." I say it over and over and over again. There is no anger in my voice, no condemnation in my tone. I simply redirect. He will not always need me to direct him back on task. Later in this book, I will cover several ways to encourage your child to focus better. But during this period of his maturation, when the inevitable wandering occurs, deal with it as graciously as a nurse deals with bedpans. It's a fact of life. You fix it and move on.

If we expect our children to be like all other children at a time when they simply can't, we lead these precious kids to believe they're a disappointment.

During this less-developed stage, we must be careful of how much damage we do. If we expect our children to be like all other children at a time when they simply can't, we lead these precious kids to believe they're a disappointment. Can you imagine berating your eighteen-month-old for an inability to read? Each day you lament his baby talk and thrust book after book in his hands waiting for him to "get it." As he grows, he has a natural desire to please you. He wants to read, he tries to read, but finds that he can't. And he is ever aware that he has greatly disappointed you. I'm sure you would agree that is obviously absurd. I have come to feel exactly the same about my son's focusing skills. Therefore, just as I would read to my young child until he is ready to read for himself, so will I constantly redirect my son's attention back to his work until his inner maturation allows him to do this for himself. Of course I want him to learn to focus on his own. He wants this too. It isn't fun for him to never accomplish what he starts out to do either. But time and constant, patient modeling are the major tools that will take us there.

Perhaps early on I worried that by taking the pressure off of him regarding all these behaviors I was simply facilitating behavior that I really ought to be discouraging. In other words, I thought if I didn't come down hard on him for allowing his mind to wander, he would never learn to focus. And what's worse, it would be my fault. I imagined him calling me on the phone when he's forty-five and saying, "Mom, I just can't focus on this bank statement. Will you bark out 'Pencil to the paper!' every few seconds while I go through it?" Well, it is with some relief that I am able report to you that he has greatly improved in his ability to focus over time. I tend to believe that time is the real factor for much of this development anyway. Maturation seems to improve most hyperactive or distractible kids. With so many pluses to these kids, we would be guilty of a significant error if we allow them to build their identity around the minuses.

Chapter 2

The Learning Environment...

or, The Best Learning Occurs While Sitting on the Table

Where your child actually works is part of the environment decision you have to make. When we first began homeschooling, I tried to re-create the school of my past, not just in how we were taught, but how it looked where we were taught. I got cute little old-fashioned desks, set up a pillowed area with lots of interesting books for reading, and placed the ABC line all around the tops of my walls of my spare bedroom now turned schoolroom. (Don't forget the school bell!) I loved the sight of my son sitting at his little desk along with another little girl I schooled at the time, with their little workbooks laid out in front of them. It was a Norman Rockwell moment. Then, as sometimes happens, the phone rang, so I left them peacefully working on their assignment. You know how the story ends, of course. From four rooms away I could hear the commotion. I excused myself from the phone call, explained the inappropriateness of their behavior, and we began again. But the situation repeated itself every time I put in a load of laundry, went to get the baby, stepped out to make lunch, and so on.

There are those who do quite well with a separate area for schooling. But for us, the best move we ever made was to the kitchen table. The washer and dryer, the food preparation area, the front door, the bathroom, and the phone are all within sight of the kitchen table. And now, so are all our school materials and the computer. During school hours, our whole world can be reached within eight steps of the kitchen table. Our desks are now relegated to a quaint antique status elsewhere in the house, and the real work happens on the big old wooden kitchen table. If you are currently schooling in the kitchen and wishing you had the space to have a separate schoolroom to minimize your child's distractions, keep in mind that you still have a house to run. You, too, have distractions. I found that teaching my son to work with the sound of me loading the dishwasher in the background is far easier than teaching him to stay focused when I leave the room.

Dealing with Distractions

In every environment there are distractions. We have lots of children in our home; our own and others we occasionally care for. There are going to be obvious distractions that are impossible for me to avoid and impossible for my son to ignore. If some of these children are working across the table from him, he is invariably more interested in what they are working on than on his own assignment. But even if the other children could be stone silent, he can still be distracted by the chance bird flitting by the window or a shadow that catches his eye on the wall. One day I remembered how much work I used to get done at those study carrels in the university library. So we put up a big tri-fold, cardboard stand-up in front of him and sort of around him. (These are often used for science fair projects and can be purchased at any teaching supplies store.) These visual blinders were a great help.

Now, the energy is not controlling the child. The child is controlling the energy.

To further develop his isolation tank, we decided that we needed "auditory blinders" as well. We found that donning a set of earphones and piping in certain types of music also kept him focused. I've heard it recommended that this sort of background music should never include music with words. And while that makes sense to me, I must tell you that some of the best music for my son is from the "Promise Keepers" albums, words and all. Mozart has also worked well for us. Harkening back to the concept that the ADHD child is always inconsistent, there will be days when music just seems to add to the stimuli and is counterproductive. Again, experiment with different music at different times. Follow your child's lead.

For the record, my son does not feel at all closed in by these constraints. He doesn't see them as a punishment resulting from his motion. On the contrary, he is relieved to finally be able to focus on his work. Now, the energy is not controlling the child. The child is controlling the energy. Now, when he feels he's having trouble focusing, he asks permission to retrieve the tape player and earphones. It gives him another tool for success. And success helps build his self-confidence.

Your Teaching Style

Another factor to the learning environment that is often overlooked but still has a strong impact is your own personal style of teaching. This one is especially tough for me. I tend to be upbeat, lively, and animated in my teaching style. For years, I was a presenter of sales seminars where such a style was an asset. For most learners, this style is simply engaging or entertaining. But for already stimulated, spirited children, that style raises their level of excitability, and with it, their level of distractibility. I recently spoke with another homeschooling mother of an ADHD child who was lamenting that her style lacked pizazz and energy. Her tone was low key, even, and calm, with no great surprises to it. It greatly uplifted her to hear that I was striving for the very style she lamented. I told her that she should see this as a gift. I found that my more animated style at times sent my son into a spin of hyper-ness that I had created. Then I expected him to simply retreat from it when a quieter learning activity came next. Thus, I have found that I must work very hard to lower my pitch, volume, speed, and spacing to accommodate a calmer and more even keeled style of teaching. If you've already got this style, see it for the advantage that it is.

Chapter 3

Put Motion in Everything You Can!

The Need to Move

When I was speaking to my son, I used to assume that if he turned upside down in his seat or began to grab frantically at imaginary flies, then he must not be listening. Wrong! If I required that he sit perfectly still and look at me intently while I spoke, he most certainly could not listen. In fact, he might implode. He needs to be moving while listening. It is this need to move that has resulted in the common observation that ADHD children often fall out of their chairs. I have seen this happen a multitude of times with my own son. My husband's grade cards from school indicate it is an inherited trait. I truly marvel at this fact. The idea of falling out of my chair is so foreign to me that I have to catch myself from laughing just at the thought of it. But it makes very clear the point that these children need to move. It is not an option for them as it is for me. The only thing I can liken it to is perhaps the feeling I get when I've held my breath for as long as I can. My insides begin to urge me gently at first and then quite violently later to make a change. That internal tension is what I imagine they are feeling all the time. If I'm right, then it's no wonder they constantly need to move.

I've read that some schools actually have two desks for their perpetual motion kids because they have accepted this need to move. Rather than wandering about when they get antsy, this second desk gives them a legitimate place to go. Other schools provide these kids with a desk but no seat so that they can stand, shift from foot to foot, move around their desk, and be in general motion without crossing a line into inappropriate behavior.

At our house, this translates into not requiring that my son constantly be in his seat while he works. He stands. He sits. He stands. He sits. He jumps. He has one foot up on the chair. He kneels on the chair. And sometimes, yes, he climbs up on the table. When I wrote this down I realizes how strange it might sound. But it came about as the result of a great learning moment we were having. It was one of those "light bulb pops on" moments that you will always relish. At the time he was talking a mile a minute, about what, I can no longer remember. As he did, he worked his way up on to the table. When he finished, I calmly said, "Look where you are." To my fascination, I watched as it dawned on him. He was completely unaware of his location until that moment.

We need to stop thinking that they are trying to ignore us or are displaying an attitude problem and simply allow them to incorporate this movement into their reception processes.

I decided at that time that it was more important to let the learning moment play itself out than it was to chastise him for being on the table. Now, I wouldn't always go that way with my decision. And mind you, I have a big old clunker of a kitchen table. There are also clear lines between what we allow in our school setting and what is considered polite behavior when out in public. Please believe me when I tell you that he has never misunderstood this and climbed on the table at the House of Hamburgers.

For many of us, it is our movement that clues people into the fact that we want to get away from some input. We shift from one foot to the other, we look away, we yawn, stretch, we tap our fingers impatiently. Moving about is what we do when we don't want to process information. But with highly spirited children, moving about is part of how they process information. We need to stop thinking that they are trying to ignore us or are displaying an attitude problem and simply allow them to incorporate this movement into their reception processes. While you may not be open to the child on the table scenario, at least, whenever possible, give your child room to move.

Now that we know these children need to move, it is our responsibility to choose the type of motion. If I allow him to choose the motion, it will almost certainly be very distracting to me or highly annoying to anyone else within range of us (i.e., other children working diligently on their workbooks). So I choose the activity. This is clearly where we've had the most fun in our schooling efforts. Whenever possible, I have involved some type of manipulative, turned our work into a game or incorporated some whole body movement. This chapter deals with adding motion to your child's work. (Games come later.) And almost everything here can be slightly altered to accommodate whatever you're working on at the moment.

Quiet Movement While Listening

There are times when you need your child to listen quietly. Some information must be imparted this way, but your child's need for movement does not go away. We often have our son doing something constructive, either related or unrelated to the information. And we find that his ears listen much better when his body is in motion.

Here are some of our favorites:

- Playing with silly putty
- Making salt dough maps or structures related to the lesson. One of the most interesting was a model of an ancient Egyptian house during one of our history lessons.
- Playing with Legos
- Screwing screws into wood
- Removing dried corn from a cob with a pair of tweezers
- Putting the plastic inserts into a Battleship game (no ships) to create a design
- Sweeping and mopping the kitchen floor (this has obvious side benefits.)
- Drawing a picture that relates to the lesson. Last week I read about the ancient Greeks and he sketched the Parthenon.
- Walking in circles around the kitchen table

- Working on a braided rug (I like this one because it could go on forever. And if he ever does finish, I'll get a pretty good-looking rug.)

Incorporating Whole Body Movement

We often play "Mother-May-I?" in our house. I ask each child an age-appropriate question. If answered correctly, the child can now progress by whatever means I choose (baby steps, giant steps, scissors walk, frog leap, etc.). Whoever reaches "Mother" first is the winner. I can easily alter my steps and questions to achieve "wins" by each player.

"Hop-on-It" works with lots of educational objectives. I put 3 x 5 cards on the floor with words on them. In one game I set out cards labeled "adjective," "noun," "verb," and "adverb." Then I call out a word, and he has to jump on the correct word type. In another version, the cards read "2," "3," "4," and "5." Then I call out 16. He has to jump on any multiple of this number. Even more fun is to have several "2's," "3's" and so on. Then when I call out 16, he has to jump on all the prime factors. If I called out "10," he would have to hop on a "5" and then a "2." If I call out "12," he would have to hop on a "2," a "3," and another "2." This game results in lots of leaping and is a good choice for burning off some excess energy.

Some other ideas with this format:

- Card types: mammal, amphibian, insect, bird, and fish.
  Call out: "I have hair." "I have live births."
- Card types: B, P, D, C, SH, PH
  Call out: the sounds made by these letters. Or a word that ends with one of these sounds.
- Card types: Cleopatra, Megiddo, Shaduf
  Call out: "I am the last Pharaoh." "I am a famous battle." "I am a simple machine."
- Card types: sternum, phalanges, patella
  Call Out: "I'm over the chest." "I'm in your foot." "I'm your kneecap."

For information that is linear, you can play "Toss-It." For very young children the alphabet is a good example. I say "A" and then throw the beanbag to him. He says "B" and then throws it back. When we've completed the alphabet we play again, but he must start with "A." We've used this game to learn the books of the Old Testament (now I finally know them!), counting by 5's, multiplication tables, and Spanish numbers.

You must be careful to have info that can be articulated quickly... Rapid return is the name of the game here.

This game can also be used for learning information in pairs, such as the abbreviations of the states. I toss and call out "Alaska," and he tosses back "AK." You must be careful to have info that can be articulated quickly. You don't want long pauses while you say, "What figure in American history is known for his penchant for long and windy speeches, and in what time period would you find him?" Toss. The rhythm of the game is lost. Rapid return is the name of the game here.

Be the Lesson

In the same vein of "whole body movement" is a concept we call "Be the Lesson." This is such a fun and positive way to learn. It simply means that you pretend to be the thing you are studying. When we studied ancient Egypt, we made a very simple Pharaoh's hat with a slot in the front. Into this slot we would put a card with a symbol for a particular pharaoh. I would wear the hat and then in dramatic fashion, act in ways that were consistent with that Pharaoh. As the children learned the Pharaohs, soon they wore the hat and did the acting.

You need to constantly ask yourself if there is any way we could *become* the items in the lesson.

They will always remember the spirited leap of a click beetle. They balled themselves up while lying on the floor, made a loud "*click*" and then leaped into the air and landed in a totally different spot, greatly confusing their predator (me).

One of our most fun examples came when we studied the anatomy of the human heart. With masking tape we made a very basic four-chambered area on the carpet of our family room. At the opening to the heart was a chute where the children lined up, waiting to enter the heart. They were pretending to be the blood on a ride through the body. The children enter one at a time through the right atrium. They tell me where they are, then, with a hug from me, they are squeezed through the valve into the right ventricle. Again, they tell me where they are. Then, they are squeezed again. Now they choose if they want to go to the right lung or the left lung. Once they are there, they pick up some oxygen (empty VCR tape boxes) and now carry it with them. The process is repeated through the left atrium and left ventricle. Next they choose where in the body (the rest of the family room) they are going to go and deposit their oxygen. They come back to the heart and wait in line. After their journey, I sat them down with a basic sketch of a body with a heart. They charted the path through the circulatory system with ease.

We've used the same basic idea in building the Tower of Babel, acting out a Greek or Roman myth, noting how a moth's wings close over its back compared to a butterfly's closing up in the air, or becoming one of several planets and orbiting around a tree, now sun, in our backyard. You need to constantly ask yourself if there is any way we could *become* the items in the lesson. Or if you're a *Magic School Bus* fan, just say, "Hmmmm, what would Ms. Frizzle do?"

Since these kids need more motion in their day, it makes sense to try to incorporate regular breaks and physical activity into your school routine. But what do you do when they clearly need an energy outlet but you don't have time for a thirty-minute walk to the park? We sometimes opt for running in place while reciting some lesson-related material. It could be the books of the Bible, times tables, or Flash Facts. (These are review questions kept on 3 x 5 cards. More on this in the section "The Many Uses of a 3 x 5 Card.") When he has worked out the majority of his wiggles, we resume.

Chapter 4

Make Many Manipulatives

Naturally there are times when you don't want your children running all over the place. Not all learning can take place while in motion. But you can still give them *something* to move, even if it's not going to be their own bodies. Children are natural manipulators, in the positive sense of the word. (I guess they're natural manipulators in the negative sense of the word too, but that is another book.) Anytime I can give them something to move while going through the assigned material, their enthusiasm for the task always continues till the end. The following methods have worked for us in learning a great variety of subjects.

Label the Picture in the Plastic Sleeve

I have a box of acetate sleeves that people use as page protectors for their reports. I simply place a drawing inside. One I have used with the younger children is of a horse. All along the edge on the outside of the sleeve are small labels I've made out of a cut up 3 x 5 card. On the back of the labels I've placed double sticky tape. The one of the horse has labels that read: muzzle, cheek, mane, shoulder, back, knee, heel, and tail. They must pull the label from the edge and place it over the correct spot. We also have one of a manger scene with eight or so labels of animals and characters. It would be easy to make a page of capital letters and then have labels of lowercase letters.

Other possibilities are:

- Shapes with labels of their word names (triangle, circle, hexagon)
- Groupings of things in different amounts and labels with numbers on them
- A giant face with labels naming the various parts (nose, eyebrow, hair)
- A map with simple parts (river, mountain, gulf, ocean)
- Human body organs (I had to trace this one!) with labels for liver, gall bladder, small intestine, etc.
- Another giant face, only this time with labels in Spanish (see Appendix A)
- A corn root aphid with labels for the many insect parts (see Appendix A)

Once, just for fun, I drew a simple bear on a half piece of poster board. Then I covered it with clear contact paper. I wrote the different parts of the bear (arm, belly, toe) with an erasable marker directly onto the contact paper. I explained to my son that each part was a "boo-boo" in need of a little bandage. Out of an old manila folder I cut bandages that were perfectly sized to cover the words on the bear. Each word on the bear had to be covered with a bandage bearing the matching word, or poor bear wouldn't heal. In the beginning, he was matching "foot" to "foot," "toe" to "toe." For a child just learning to visually discriminate the difference between letters, this is a great exercise. After the child has progressed to early reading, I change the bear. The words on the bear are erased. Now, instead of the word appearing where his "boo-boo" is located, he now sports only an "x." The child must actually read the word on the bandage and locate the correct spot on the bear.

Note: The smaller label games are good take-along activities for in the car—no pencils to "accidentally" fall out of reach.

Candles and Their Flames

I created a master form of eight candles sitting in eight candle holders. I made lots of copies so that these were consumable. Then I cut out eight flames from some old yellow paper. On the bottom of each candle holder I wrote the item that would be paired with a flame. On each flame I wrote the corresponding item. When the child finds the correct flame to go with the correct candle, he glues it to the top. This exercise can be used for any information that can be paired.

- coins to their values
- Latin roots to their meanings
- separate parts of a compound word

- numbers that paired together equal 100
- states and their capital cities

Stickers: Relief for Tired Hands

On a day when we have done a lot of cursive writing or copying of spelling lists, I sometimes use stickers to give those hands a break. Stickers can be purchased inexpensively at any office supply store. This is especially good for the child who is just learning to write. Fine motor skills take time to develop and until they do, that little hand tires easily.

In a math workbook, if there are twenty problems, get twenty little circle stickers and write the answers on them in a random fashion. Have the child scan the page of stickers, find the appropriate one, and stick it on the answer blank. The child still has to figure out the problem. The goal of learning the math is still achieved. This is just fun. So even on days when there isn't a heavy load of writing, using the stickers can help maintain your child's interest in the lesson longer than if he or she were simply writing the answers.

> **Fine motor skills take time to develop and until they do, that little hand tires easily.**

Feeding the Seals

This is a good game for any group of items that can be placed under one heading. Start with a plain letter-sized envelope. Cut a rectangular piece of plain or light-colored paper that is four inches by nine inches. Round off the corners on one side. Glue this to the back side of the closing flap of the envelope. Now, open the envelope and draw very wide lips, putting the top lip on the lifted flap of the envelope and the bottom lip on the body of the envelope. Draw on remaining features.

You can decide just what this seal eats. Some of my seals will eat only adjectives. Some will eat only things that start with the letter "B." Some will eat only things that rhyme with the word "TIP." Write on the bottom section of your seal what his dietary requirements are. If you don't want to have a different set of seals for each topic you wish to cover, then cover the bottom section of the seal in clear tape. Now you can write on them

with erasable pens. Next, take 3 x 5 cards and draw a simple picture or write the word for your particular seal's diet. I usually give my children three seals with a stack of cards (which we call fish) to feed the seals. The stack of cards—I mean fish—are given to the child in an envelope appropriately called "The Fish Bucket," with a simple drawing of a bucket on the front with a few fish jumping out of the water.

Some items that can be used with the seals are:

- Adjectives, nouns, adverbs
- Pacific Northwest, New England States, Midwest (using cards of different states)
- Iroquois, Cherokee, Hurons (cards listing things specific to each tribe)
- Mammals, reptiles, fish (The cards I use for feeding the seals here might simply have an animal listed or might have characteristics of the three groups, such as "breathes by taking oxygen from the water.")
- True, False (review any subject with true or false statements. Example: Thomas Jefferson signed the Magna Carta, Noah lived inside the whale for three days)
- 1 syllable, 2 syllables, 3 syllables (cards with words containing 1, 2, or 3 syllables)
- Ten, Sixteen, Thirty (Have a stack of cards with simple addition problems where the answer will always be one of three answers. This exercise can obviously be used for subtraction, and so on.)

Deliver the Mail

A much simpler idea than the seals, but usable in exactly the same way, is an exercise I call "Deliver the Mail." I simply take a piece of paper and divide it into four sections. In each section I draw a very simple house. I make each house look a little different just to make it interesting. On each house I write the type of house that it is (the category). For instance, I might put a different number on each house to designate how many syllables a word contains. I point to the house with the "3" on the front and make clear to the child that this house can only receive mail that has three syllables in it. Then in an envelope I put cut-up pieces of paper upon which have been written various words. This group of words is the "mail" that needs to be delivered. The child simply needs to lay the correct mail on the correct house. If you want to really make it fun, put a slot in the house with a little paper catcher on the back so they can actually slide the mail into the door. Be sure to include a little opening in your catcher bag on the back of the page. Otherwise, you'll be forced to get the mail out by rerouting it back through the little slot.

The Many Uses of a 3 x 5 Card

You have probably figured out by now that I am fond of 3 x 5 cards. But for good reason. They are instant manipulatives that have an endless number of uses, and they are cheap. I buy them inexpensively in stacks of 1,000. My children sit for long periods of time on the floor of the family room matching and rematching cards. There are so many uses for these cards. I'm always amazed at how soon I need another stack. Here are just a few games:

"Going Fishing" is any game that involves a stick with a string tied on the end and a magnet on the end of the string that picks up "fish" from off of the floor (3 x 5's with a paperclip on them). I don't know why this thrills children, but any set of problems seems to be accomplished with great enthusiasm when the answers lie on the undersides of these fish. You can get fancy and cut out fish shapes or draw fish on the backs, but I've discovered that children are more delighted by the fishing process rather than the realism of the fish itself. When I was teaching color words, I had a rainbow picture for them to color in. Each fish had a different color written on its underside. The child would pull up the card, read the color, and everyone would color in that section of the rainbow.

Another version of the game involves a rainbow divided into rectangular sections (see Appendix A). In this case, the fish have to be hidden somehow so the kids cannot see which fish they are catching. They catch two fish. On the underside of the fish is a number. After catching two fish, they add the numbers together and color in the section with the corresponding answer. This game can go on a long time, as they will often repeat numbers they have gotten before. I've added sections that contain a star. When they get a repeated number, they fill in one of these sections. So even for a number that appears more than once they still have something to do.

"Spanish Lock & Key Colors" is a matching game that teaches colors in Spanish. I used 3 x 5's cut in half for this to save money, but you could use a full card. On one half I drew a simple looking lock. On the lock I wrote a color in Spanish. On the other half I drew a simple looking key and colored it in with a color I wanted them to learn. The child matches the right key with the right lock.

"Matching Uppercase and Lowercase Letters" is a natural for younger children with 3 x 5's. You create a set of cards with capital letters and another set with lowercase letters. We call these "Mommy" letters and "baby" letters. I give the child both stacks, and her job is to match each Mommy with her correct baby. For some reason this task is more fun if the matched set is joined together with a paper clip.

"Learning Coins, Their Names and Their Values" is the object in this game. On one set of cards write the words "penny," "nickel," "dime," and "quarter." On another set write the values for each. Have the child match them up. As your child becomes more skilled with money, use rubber stamps to put several coins on each card. (A set of these stamps can be purchased at most teaching supply stores.) Have the amount totals on other cards and have the children match them.

"The Sentence Detective" is a game to help children pay attention to sentence structure. Take a simple sentence. Write it down on a set of cards, putting one card for each word of the sentence. Mix them up. Tell your child that she must be a good detective and figure out

The Sentence Detective

the best sentence using the clues on the cards. The mixed-up versions can be pretty silly. In fact, your child may find more delight in creating the most absurd sentence possible with the words provided. Allow the fun, but make sure she also gets the original sentence.

"Flip Cards" allow your child to practice any word ending along with several beginning letters or even blends. It involves using one full-sized card for the letters that end the word and then several cards placed on top of the card for different beginnings. In the example below, on the full-sized card you see the letters "in." On top of the full-sized card are thirteen half cards with letter blends such as "sh," "th," "ch" and letters such as "s," "b," and "f." Next, punch the upper left corner of all of the cards and then join them with those little key chains that can be picked up at any teachers' store. So your child flips and says, "shin, thin, chin, sin," etc.

"Cards Into Envelopes" is a simpler version of "Feed the Seals." There is no cute seal face envelope. When I was trying to teach my daughter to do simple counting I used this method. I started with a stack of 3 x 5's upon which I had drawn simple shapes, such as triangles, simple butterflies, or stars. Ten of the cards have five things on them. Ten more of the cards have four things on them. I also have similar cards with groupings of three, two, and one. I have ten of each number type, so there are fifty in all. There are also five envelopes. One envelope has the number five on it. Another, the number four, and so on. I then

mix the 3 x 5 cards. The child picks up a card, counts the objects on it, and places it in the correct envelope.

"Pick It Up" is a name I use for any game where the object is to pick up one of the many cards laid out in front of a student. This is a good option for drilling on multiplication or division.

I place cards on the table with practice problems on them, such as "3 x 6," "7 x 4," "9 x 9," and "12 x 5." I usually have at least ten cards on the table that he can choose from. Then I call out products: "81." "28." We time how long it takes us to go through a set, and then we attempt to beat our last time. You can also reverse the procedure by having the problems in your hand and have your child search for the answers from the table cards.

My son struggles with alphabetizing because he can't remember what comes next in the alphabet without reciting from the beginning. So in the game **"Alphabetizing Pick-Up,"** the cards on the table have various letters on them. The easier way to play this game is to call out the letters on either side of the card letter. For example, if "M" is on the table, I call out, "Find the letter between 'L' and 'N.'" A slightly harder version is to call out the letter immediately before. The hardest version is to say, "Which letter is four letters after 'I'?" Then, they need to know groups of four in their head. This exercise is similar to having a long poem memorized but being able to pull out and recite an individual line.

> **I am working so hard to get this information into his head while his brain is letting it all leak out through the natural course of being human.**

If your child has problems alphabetizing, write several words on 3 x 5's and have him put them in order. It is much easier than looking at a list of words and holding a word in his head while he continues to scan the list deciding if there is another word that should precede it. I developed another use for 3 x 5's to combat the naturally occuring "brain drip" that plagues us all.

I have often wished that I remembered more of the things I learned in school. We all have lamented the zillions of facts we once learned for a test, only to have them drift out of our memory within days. Oh, the stuff we once knew! While many of the facts I've forgotten really haven't hindered my path through life in any way, others I've often wished that I had retained. Many items would have been a wonderful framework upon which to place new information or make sense of a new event.

I saw the same erosion of knowledge happening in my son's education, and it bothered me somewhat. First of all, I am working so hard to get this information into his head while his brain is letting it all leak out through the natural course of being human. Second, it would be much nicer for him in the future years, when he hears about a great event in history, if he already has a basic framework on which to hang all of the new information. What a waste to have learned all this cool stuff only to have to relearn it again later. Luckily, I remembered a useful piece of folk wisdom. "If you don't use it, you lose it."

So how do you "use" interesting details about ancient Egypt in the twenty-first century? The way we accommodate this is through "Flash Facts." These are simply cards with key information from our studies posed as questions on the front with the answers on the backs. As we cover new material, I simply make up a card for items I think are worth retaining. Then we rip through these every so often for review. We have "Flash Facts" on history, astronomy, grammar, rules of math and spelling, insects, and geography, among others. Even a year later, he can tell me the functions of spiracles on an insect and the important lesson learned by the Egyptians from their temporary captors, the Hyksos. And the best part of it is now I can tell you too!

Chapter 5

There's a Game in There Somewhere

Games are a natural extension of a child's love of motion. They may know they are learning something, but they are having so much fun that they don't care. You may be thinking that it would be impossible to create a game to play every day. Yes, that would be true if you had to actually develop and create one for each item you want to cover. But many of these games are simply blank forms that are reusable every day. Here are some of our favorites:

"BINGO Blanks"

If you've ever played a Lotto or Jingo game, you've basically played a version of the ever popular BINGO. There are scores of these games in teaching supply stores. But they cost around $10 or more per game. I knew we could use the concept for a number of educational areas in our schooling, but I didn't want to buy a game for each area. I also didn't want to make a separate game for each subject. The solution was to create blank BINGO game boards that could be used over and over again for a variety of subjects.

Start with a large colored sheet of construction paper. Cut it in half. Take a 3 x 5 card and draw lines on it that divide the card into eight boxes. Glue the card onto the construction paper. You can decorate the area around the 3 x 5 with stickers or pictures cut from old work-books. I simply drew large block letters that spelled out B-I-N-G-O and put them along the top. Now cover your card in clear tape. After having experimented with several tapes, I have developed a strong preference for the Premium Heavy Duty Box Sealing Tape, a 3M product made under the Scotch name brand. Other brands often won't work with an erasable marker. Or they are so flimsy that they fly about when you're working with them and often ruin the piece you've created.

Covering your piece will obviously add greatly to its longevity. The main purpose is to allow you to write in the blanks with erasable markers. (Vis-A-Vis makes a good quality fine point.)

The residual adhesive on the non-sticky side left over from its contact with the sticky side can sometimes make for poor marking. We've found that the markers make a clearer, cleaner line on your tape if you wipe off your tape once with a good ammonia-containing cleaner before you start playing. Make several blank boards.

Let's say you are going to play a game to learn body organs. On one board you will write the name of one organ in each of the eight boxes on the playing card. On another board, you will write eight more organs. Some will be the same as the previous board, but some will be new. Next you will need to make the calling cards. On each one of these write the definition of each of the organs. Now shuffle them and call them out one at a time. The first might read, "I am the organ of the body that is full of millions of small sacs that can pull oxygen from the air." The child searches their board for the square containing the word "lung."

Now, you have to choose some object to be a marker when your child finds one of the sought after items on his card. You can cut more colored pieces of paper into squares or circles. Again, consider covering the front and back of each shape with tape to increase its life, especially since these will be handled so much more. You can also use household items as markers: pennies, big paper clips, buttons, etc. These markers add a manipulative to the process and make it more interesting. But keep in mind that these boards are tape-covered. Your child can simply mark off his box when he has a match. Not only does this alleviate the need to find an item to use as a marker, but you won't have to worry about pennies being bumped off the board in a moment of excitement.

Because there are only eight blocks per board, you can play a shorter game with younger kids. You simply play until someone's board is full. If you have only one child, you become the other player. I have found that when we are covering more difficult mate-rial, the younger kids still want to play for the sake of the fun, and they are exposed to a lot of new information in the process. With older kids we usually have them take two or even more boards to play at a time. For this reason, you will want to have on hand at least two boards per child, if not more.

We have used this game in learning American Sign Language. The cards have words such as "tree," "mother," "day," and so on. I have a separate set of cards in a pile from which I draw to determine what I will sign to them next. This method can really be used for teaching any information, such as:

- Any historical figures. The cards contain interesting information about each person.
- Symbols for the elements (C, B, Au) The cards have the full name (Carbon, Boron, Gold).
- Vocabulary words. The cards contain the definitions.
- Rhyming words. The cards contain simple words they rhyme with.
- States. The cards tell interesting details about the states (state capital, state flower, etc.).

You can make your game boards more detailed and narrow in focus if you like. We have a fun one about insects. I drew a large beetle on a sheet of paper. On its back are sixteen boxes. I made several copies and then had the kids color in the beetle's body. In the boxes I've written in pencil the words to be used with this game (you'll see an example in Appendix A). After they are mastered, I can easily erase the pencil and change the words. Some of the words on our current game are "camouflage," "thorax," "entomology," "spiracles," and "habitat." I keep each beetle in a plastic sleeve, and the kids mark them off with an erasable marker just as discussed above.

"Bear Belly Bingo"

At one point I had three kids who needed to improve their fine motor skills. But only one of them enjoyed copying letter after letter after letter. I needed a fun game that would get them to practice the motions used in writing letters and yet avoid the "write-three-lines-of-the-letter-Q" philosophy. The answer was a game we call "Bear Belly Bingo," because it is played on the belly of a large bear. You will need to make calling chips, design cards, and the "Bear Belly Bingo" game boards on which the children actually write. It is best if you create your main Bear Belly Bingo design and then make lots of copies that can be used. You can also copy the sample in Appendix A. The reason I prefer consumable papers to my usual tape-covered items used with erasable markers is because the goal in this game is to practice writing, or at least the many strokes used in making letters. While in most other instances, tape-covered, erasable games would be preferred, in this case I prefer they get the feel of pencil on paper as part of the process.

For the game board, draw a grid containing sixteen squares in a 4 x 4 manner. Across the top put the letters "B-E-A-R," and along the side put the numbers "1-2-3-4." This provides a cross-referencing system for finding the correct square.

Now you need to make sixteen little calling chips. Use anything you can write call references on (such as "B-2" or "R-4"). I used little plastic chips with the metal rims that you see in magnet sets, because I got a bag of about 300 of them at a garage sale for twenty-five cents. But you can use little circles of paper or popsicle sticks, or whatever you can find that will take a sticker or a mark from your pen. I put a little sticker circle on one side and wrote the coordinates on each one. There should be sixteen calling chips. You need to make as many complete sets of chips as you will have children playing the game at the same time.

> **You decide how the game is to be won. Change it every time you play to keep it interesting.**

In other words, if you have five children playing, you will need five sets.

Next, pull out one chip from one set for one child. Then pull out a second chip from the second set for the second child. They both have their coordinates. And both coordinates are different. Have them locate the correct box on their "Bear Belly Bingo" playing board and wait for your instruction. Now you flip over the design card. On the design card they will see what design they are to put into that box. The designs vary. One card might be filled with small circles. Another might have a row of five wavy lines. The point of these cards is to practice the same motions children use in making letters, but to do it in a way that does not remind them at all of writing.

You decide how the game is to be won. It may be when someone has four in a row. It may be when someone has four in a box fashion. It may be when someone has filled all four corners. Change it every time you play to keep it interesting.

"Vicky Velpanoid from Venus" or How to Make Flash Cards Fun

I was tutoring an eight-year-old boy for a time, and we were using flash cards for some of our work. He really needed the drill, but he grew weary of the repetition. I noted that he had a fascination with anything weird—monster books, beings from outer space, and the like. So one day I drew up a rather odd-looking creature standing beside her spaceship and dubbed her "Vicky Velpanoid," from Venus. In the spaceship were eight rectangular areas that we called her "fuel pods." We had another one called "Milnerd Moonman" (check them out in Appendix A). Same idea.

Now that I had his interest, we went through the flash cards. When he got five in a row, he had a "pod." He would move the cards off to his side of the table and color in one of the empty pods. If he got three in a row and then missed one, the cards were mine, and I put them at the bottom of my pile. He had lost his pod. But, of course, he always got another one. And eventually Vicky was able to return to her Venus home.

Another version of this game is for each of you to have an alien page. You can be Vicky, he can be Milnerd. If he gets three in a row right, he has a pod. But each time he gets one wrong, it goes on your pile. When you have three on your pile, you get a pod. It's a race to see which alien gets to go home first. I strongly urge you to choose your amounts carefully so that the child is destined for victory. Learning games are not much fun if the teacher always wins.

Products Worth Considering

I hesitate to recommend buying games for several reasons. Money is often tight for homeschoolers, and even when money is not tight, I still am. It bothers me to spend money on a game that has only one use. When the kids tire of the game, that $25 game just sits there in a beautiful cardboard box and is seldom opened again. Lastly, so many wonderful games can be made with paper, pencil, and the occasional need for glue that I find myself almost never buying a game anymore.

> **I strongly urge you to choose your amounts carefully so that the child is destined for victory. Learning games are not much fun if the teacher always wins.**

There are, however, some games that have overcome these objections and are worth considering. One we have enjoyed is called *Fun Thinkers Books* to be used with the *Fun Thinkers Match-Frame* by Educational Insights. There are at least ten books from which to select, and they cover a wide range of topics for ages 4-12. There are books at three different skill levels, and each book has over twenty-one different matching games in it. Each page in a book has sixteen squares in it that match in some way to a square on the opposite page. It is used with a set of plastic squares that rest in a two-piece, hinged, framed grid that sets on the pages. In our house we call this "working with tiles." On the back of each tile is a color so that when your child has finished his matching, he closes the frame, flips it over, and compares it to the color guide at the top of the page. If the color pattern matches, he knows he's done it right. If not, he has to figure out where he went wrong.

When I purchased these books, they were less than $6 each. Considering the fact that there are over twenty games per book and that we have used them consistently for years with each child, they were well worth the investment.

A second purchase I have not regretted has been a book called *Polyhedra Dice Games*, published by Ideal School Supply Company. This book has game pages that you can copy and are played with a set of dice that you must buy separately. The cost of the dice is minimal. The book has forty math games in it. It starts with five games for learning numeration, fifteen for addition, then on through subtraction, multiplication, division, mixed operations, fractions and decimals, geometry, measurement, and graphing. We have been using this book for years and have yet to exhaust this resource. When I purchased the book it was only $12.50. If I tried to create forty such games on my own, I would have used up $12.50 just in tape.

I own a series of books that I find myself constantly recommending to people. They are written by a teacher named Peggy Kaye. They are titled *Games for Math, Games for Reading, Games for Writing,* and *Games for Learning.* There are over fifty games in each book, most of which require no more than paper and pencil. Ms Kaye has clearly tried these games, and has all the kinks worked out of them. It is from these books that I found "Roadblock," the game that has become such a pillar in our reading program. (More on this is found in the chapter entitled "Phind the Phun in Phonics.") The games are very well organized so that you can peruse the index and find a new game that meets the current need in your child's education. They are designed for children from kindergarten through third grade. I have seen them in several libraries. When I purchased mine they cost $14.00 each. If you can prove you are homeschooling, some book stores will give you a discount. In our area, Borders gives a 20% discount to educators only on educational material. Our local homeschooling association provides cards for proof of membership that I have used for this purpose. I have also used my Home School Legal Defense Association card for verification.

Another book I purchased years ago and would never part with is called *Games: Tools for Learning* by Janice and Mark Vreeland. If you've ever visited a vendor hall at a state homeschool conference, you may have seen them there. However, I think a lot of people walk by this product because it lacks the flash and packaging of the surrounding tables stacked with slick, multicolored products. That is truly unfortunate, for it is a gold mine of gaming ideas. Not only do they give easy directions for making specific games, there are plenty of grids and basic forms you can use to create any game. When I met Janice Vreeland five years ago, at that point she had created nearly 1,000 games from the designs clearly outlined in this book. I credit her book with greatly encouraging the change in our early homeschooling efforts from rote and drill to fun and games. The book was then and is still now $24.95 and can be purachased directly from the Vreelands by calling 414-327-4288.

One other product we've really enjoyed is called *Calc-U-Draw*, published by Buki Ltd. I cannot tell you that this is reusable or even an exceptional value. But it has provided an occasional delightful break from the math workbook. Each of the eighteen pages has lots of math problems on them. The answers to these problems are then plotted on the grid on the same page. When the dots on the grid are connected in order, they create a picture. My son loves these. It makes math seem to have a purpose for him. There are several levels from which to choose. When I purchased ours they were $3.99 for a tablet containing eighteen sets of math problems and grids. This comes out to about twenty-two cents per page. I guess I figured since we don't do the candy machines in the grocery stores, I'll allow this.

Chapter 6

Phind the Phun in Phonics!

This chapter could easily go into the gaming section of this book. But one particular game has been such a big part of our schooling and has carried so much weight in the learning process in our house that it deserves a chapter of its own. Without question, the most useful and versatile game we have in our teaching repertoire is called "Roadblock." It can be used for the most basic introduction of the alphabet and for more advanced information, such as naming human bones. I discovered it in a book called *Games for Learning*, by Peggy Kaye. It has been the core of our learning-to-read program. The basics of this sound so simple you won't believe it can achieve the results that it does.

You simply create a game board with many slots. (It should not be covered with tape.) Ours has twenty spaces, but yours can have fifteen or twenty-five, whatever the appropriate challenge would be for your child. We drew a roadway with a gas station near the start area and a little house along the way (see our version in Appendix A). If you're just starting to expose your child to letters, you start by putting ten or so letters in the spaces, repeating each letter somewhere in the "road" once. Now your child selects a little car and gasses it up at the pump, invoking whatever "filling the tank" sounds they deem appropriate. When they're ready, they start down the road by attempting to name the first letter. If correct, they progress. When they get stuck, I put up a roadblock. (We have an actual little plastic roadblock that adds a nice touch, but you can just as easily drop your hand down in karate-chop fashion after the difficult letter.) We go over the difficult letter several times and in several ways. (More detailed tips on teaching letters and their sounds are found later in this chapter.) Then they have to start over at the beginning. When they get to the difficult letter, they take great delight in being able to "crash" through the roadblock. I only allow three roadblocks per game. If they don't make it after that, we put it away until tomorrow. If your child completes an entire journey on the first try, you need to increase the level of difficulty. I try to aim for a difficulty level that requires about three tries to

My son's last phonics-related Roadblocks contained the words "psychologist," "hydrochloric," "dodecahedron," "echolocation," "cumulus," "tintinnabulation" and "atrophy." It was somewhere at this point that I determined that he had a pretty good grasp of phonics.

achieve. When they complete one game, I make a new roadblock and incorporate some of the letters that gave them trouble in the last game.

This game can be used for any age child and at any stage of reading. After letter names we went to letter sounds. When it was time to move on to simple words, I would always introduce the letters of the word, in order, in the squares immediately preceding the new word. For example, if we are going to work on the word "am," then the first square contains the letter "a," followed by a square containing the letter "m." In the very next square is the word "am." Now I ask the child to make the sounds individually again while looking at the word, and then we attempt to "squish" the sounds together. The next stage is to move on to simple two- or three-letter, phonetically pure words, and so on. My son's last phonics-related Roadblocks contained the words "psychologist," "hydrochloric," "dodecahedron," "echolocation," "cumulus," "tintinnabulation" and "atrophy." It was somewhere at this point that I determined that he had a pretty good grasp of phonics. (P.S. This was in the second grade.) So we continued to use the game format and shifted to identifying Latin roots, reciting vocabulary definitions, giving the location of particular human bones, etc. With my daughter we've just started using it for recognizing cursive letters.

Knowing the sounds of letters is still quite a distance from being able to read words. Some kids make this leap so easily that the milestone is hardly noticeable. But other kids struggle forever in what is called the "decoding" stage. In this stage, they do not see the word as a unit. They still sound out every indi-vidual sound. And yet they cannot push the sounds together into a word. They don't hear how these separate sounds could possibly blend together.

> **Knowing the sounds of letters is still quite a distance from being able to read words.**

Down to the Details

Now that you've got a general idea of how the game works, here are some nitty-gritty details on how to cover the right material in a step-wise fashion so that your child finds the game fun and challenging but not overwhelming.

First level—Learning the Letters

Put ten or so letters of the alphabet on the first Roadblock. Since our game had twenty spaces, we obviously repeated each letter twice somewhere on the gameboard.

My personal preference is to begin with the capital letters in order to avoid confusion between the lower case "p," "d," "q," and "b." (Although research has been somewhat var-ied, my opinion is that capital letters are still easier to distinguish.) In the capital letters, your child may have trouble distinguishing the "M" from the "W." A little trick we used to clarify this was to point out that the "M" had two mountain peaks and the "W" could hold water.

During this stage the goal for your child is to simply learn the name of each letter, not its sound. If your child seems to struggle with a particular letter, see that this letter appears two or three times in the next Roadblock. Continue making new games until he or she is comfortable with naming any letter of the alphabet on sight.

At some point, you will need to introduce lower case letters. Refer to the game, "Candles and Their Flames" for suggestions on how to teach the pairs of upper-and lower-case letters. Don't bury your children, however, under the weight of having to learn all the letter types before they can move on to the fun of learning to read.

Second level—Learning the Sounds

You can use the exact same Roadblocks for this game that you created in level one. But now instead of naming the letters, the child will name the letter *and* tell you what sound goes with each letter.

Teach only one sound per letter at this point. For example, when teaching the letter "c," do not introduce the "s" sound that is sometimes given it, as in *cereal*. Stick with the hard sound for now. The same goes for "g"; hard g's only for now. "Germ," or the soft "g" sound, comes later.

As for vowels, stick with the short sound. "A" as in "apple," "E" as in "Ed," and "I" as in "itch," "O" as in "octopus;" "U" as in "umbrella." Long vowels and silent letters will eventually become part of the process, but not for two more levels.

Special note: With whatever phonics program you choose, be very careful of the sounds you assign to the letters. The insidious "uhhhh" that people often add to letter sounds creates so much unnecessary confusion in your child's phonics lessons. The sound for "p" is NOT "puhhh." It is an almost staccato "p." The sound for "g" is not "guhhh." If you always add "uhs" to the sounds you teach, your children will think "pig" is pronounced "puh-ih-guh." And rightly so if they've been taught the incorrectly drawn-out sound for many letters. Keep the sounds short and accurate, and the efforts to "squish" them will go much more easily.

Also, be sure to teach the "x" sound as a "ks," like a shortened "kiss." I don't care how many times you have seen "xylophone" in a store-bought alphabet game, don't teach "x" as the "z" sound that it rarely is. Your child is much more likely to want to read *fox* and *six* and *ax* than they are to want to read *xylophone*.

Continue making Roadblocks with letters until your child is comfortable giving the sound for each letter on sight.

Third level—Starting to Squish

This is the part that your child finds most exciting. The complicated mystery of reading starts to unravel for them right here. Don't rush it. Keep it fun.

> **The complicated mystery of reading starts to unravel for them right here. Don't rush it. Keep it fun.**

While your board may have, say, twenty spaces available, you should not throw twenty new words at your child with each new Roadblock. Rather, your child should learn about five or six new words per Roadblock. For example, let's say you want to introduce the word *cap*. Your first space will contain just the letter "c." The second space will have an "a" in it, and the third space will have a "p." This will provide a review of all the needed sounds immediately before the actual word *cap* shows up in the fourth space.

When your child gets to the space with the full word *cap* in it, he or she may want to pronounce *cap* by articulating each individual sound again, and will call that "reading." This is the point when you need to encourage your child "squish" the sounds together. Some children will get this almost immediately, and some children will need more time and encouragement.

With some of the kids I have tutored, I've found that singing the vowel sound sometimes helps. I start by explaining that without vowels there would be no singing. We test this theory by trying to sing some consonants. The letters "k" and "t" clearly cannot carry a tune. (Okay so "m" and "n" can be sung or at least hummed. But you get the idea.) So after a few giggles, we now sing some vowel sounds. "Ahhh" and "Ohhh" can carry a melody anywhere you want to take it. Vowel sounds carry a singer's words.

Now we try it with a simple word…*pig*. You hit the consonant "p," then you sing the "i" sound by drawing it out ridiculously long, and then hit the last consonant "g."

P—ihhhhh——g

It is important that they sing that middle vowel sound until they end it with the "g." They should strive to have no breaks between the singing and the final sound. Having drawn out the sound and then cutting it off with the next sound, they begin to feel and hear the blending. Soon they can blend the letters with little effort, and the singing is a thing of the past.

> **With some of the kids I have tutored, I've found that singing the vowel sound sometimes helps.**

Continue working on this level until your child can easily "squish" any phonetically pure word that you place in front of them. By phonetically pure, I mean any word that follows the clear letter sounds you have laid out thus far. In other words, if you've said that "f" always has the airy "fffff" sound as in *feather*, don't suddenly include the word *of*, in which f has a "v" sound. Stick to the rules you've laid out.

Fourth level—Partner Sounds

Hopefully by now your child has mastered a basic set of phonics rules that will serve him well in reading much of the English language. Now it's time to learn some of the variations. In this level, your children will start to learn that letters sometimes have sounds other than the ones he's already learned. He will learn that a letter may have a group of "partner" sounds that can go with a letter. For example, while "g" often has a hard sound, as in *goat*, it can also have a soft sound, such as in *giraffe* and *giant*. Likewise, the letter "s," will usually have the same sound as found at the beginning of the word *sock*, but is sometimes pronounced more like a "z," as in *cause*.

This is also an appropriate time to explain the long vowel sounds. In our house, we always said that vowels can sometimes sound like their names. For example, you might explain that the letter "e", which has up until now been pronounced "eh," has a partner sound of "eeee." In the next Roadblock, then, include words such as "me," "he," "be," and so on. Try to intoduce only one new sound per Roadblock, and then intersperse these new words with some of the good old phonetically pure words.

(See the following sections for a starter list of words that is appropriate for this level.)

This is also the time when I introduce children to some common blends, like "sh," "th," "ch," and "wh." In the beginning, I always underline these blends when they occur, to remind these budding readers that there is something new here, and also to guide them in thinking of these two letters as a unit rather than as two separate components.

This is the section where I introduce the silent "e" that is often found at the end of words. When there is an "e" at the end of a word, we cover it up with our thumb and basically ignore it. But, we go back to the previous vowel and realize that the silent "e" has made this first vowel "go long." In other words, this vowel will be pronounced like its name. For example, in the word "tape," we would cover up the final "e." Now when the child looks at what is left, she might be tempted to pronounce it "tap," like in "map." Make her track backwards from the covered silent "e" to the previous vowel—the "a"—and say out loud that now this vowel has "gone long" and must be pronounced like its name.

Lastly, you should introduce your child to words that are affectionately called "sight" words, because they must be recognized simply on sight. In other words, they don't follow the rules. Yet most children's literature would be completely unreadable if your child didn't know some of the most common sight words. My favorite is *said*. With our previously-learned phonics rules it would have been pronounced "saaaaaaahhhh-eeeeeee-d." "Sed" would have been a more apt spelling. Nonetheless, it must be learned along with other rebellious spellings like *do, was, is, the* and so on. Sometimes, remembering the pronunciation of these maverick words can be encouraged with simple rhymes. We made up a little poem for the word *the* because it caused one child so much trouble:

T - H - E, T - H - E
That spells the, *a word for me.*
The dog, the cat, the bird, the tree
All start with the, *T - H - E.*

Fifth Level—Taking it to the Limit

Once you are comfortable with the basic format of the game, you may want to locate a commonly-used word list as a guide. Find one you like from the many that are out there. But don't miss another great option found on your child's own bookshelves. Pick a simple book from your child's collection and use it as a resource to fill in your Roadblock for a few days. When you are done, your child now has a book that she can read from cover to cover. You could also take the total words that your child can already read and put them together in her own book which she can illustrate. You will eventually reach a point where your child will recognize most basic words. Some children will need more spelling rules at this point, and others are such visual learners that the transition from this point to all other types of words in the English language is seamless. To find words of greater difficulty, I cracked open a dictionary. (Just make sure to keep pronunciation lessons and vocabulary lessons distinct from one another.) While the words "funambulist," "cryohydrate," and "hemidemisemiquaver" are highly unlikely to appear in any typical piece of children's literature, being able to pronounce them certainly boosts the self-image of a young reader.

The Teacher's Store at Our House

This game became so very popular in our house, I think, partially because I took Peggy Kaye's above game a step further. I made little plastic credit cards for each child.

(White 3 x 5 card cut to shape of real credit card, cute sticker of child's choice put in center, child's name on top, clear tape on both sides.) After playing Roadblock, they had to count up how many spaces they had traversed. Each space equals one cent on their card. Their money is added to whatever amount currently on their credit card. As they spend their money, the adjusted amount is recorded anew on their credit card.

Now they can take their "money" and spend it in our little Teacher's Store. I set up a small shelf in my kitchen filled with doodads (mostly garage sale finds), some candy, and a few items I knew they'd really work for. The store only opens once a day. You can't believe what these children will do to shop in this store! If I forget to do the Roadblock game, the four-year-olds will loudly object until my memory is seriously jogged.

There are many educational objectives accomplished in this setup. The younger children get experience in counting the squares afterward. As they grow older, they can add the new points to the accumulated points left from before, and then they can subtract them as they spend them. They are also learning the important consumer-spending lesson that if you want something "big" you have to save for it.

Chapter 7

It's Monday Morning, How Do I Teach...?

Math

Let's talk about *math workbooks*. The first question you may be pondering is why even use a math workbook. Aren't they the worst possible things for the highly distractible child? "Fill in that blank! Read this section! Sit in your chair and complete sections A, B, and C." The kid doesn't even get to move around. So why use them? Good question. And in a perfect world I would be so incredibly creative and have so much time that I would have no workbooks anywhere in our house. Learning would be this natural process that occurs in the course of a day where I surround my children with a rich environment, organized around a week or two of intense focusing on a unit of study, say the silkworm industry. We would measure the length of a strand of silk that we unwound from one of the many silkworms we had raised. We would calculate just how many pounds of leaves our 2,300 worms would eat to produce the thirty-five yards of fabric that we wove. And we would decipher the shipping rates used for several geographic time zones in the world to where silk is then shipped.

Perhaps your world can accommodate such a prodigious effort, but on a typical morning in my world, I'm still trying to calculate how much coffee to put into the filter if I'm trying to reuse half from the last batch due to a 25% increase in the cost of coffee from last year's prices. While I truly believe in the unit study approach and throw heaps of applause upon those who school in this manner, you will find workbooks in our house. While I incorporate the unit study method whenever I can because of its great learning value, I still find that I need workbooks, particularly in math and language, to maintain a continuity and to avoid gaps. But I must admit that I also have them because there are days when I haven't a creative bone in my body or an ounce of energy. And yet I know that school must go on. I have found that I am not alone in this and that many other homeschooling parents do the same. Therefore, the answer to your question about why I would devote any time to making workbooks fun is because so many of us use them.

> **One of the easiest ways to turn a section of math problems into a game is to make a quick puzzle out of it.**

A Workbook Exercise Turned Puzzle

One of the easiest ways to turn a section of math problems into a game is to make a quick puzzle out of it. My son dives into his math problems whenever I do this.

Take a piece of letter-sized paper. On one side, write the answers to a set of math problems (approximately ten). Scatter the answers about on the page in random fashion. On the flip side of the page, write a note about how special your child is, or give directions to find a secret treasure hidden in the house. Then get out your scissors and start cutting out each of the math answers, shaping each piece in a unique, puzzle-like shape.

Now spread the items all over the floor answer side up. When your child completes the first math problem, he picks up the piece with the matching answer. He flips the piece over and discovers one small piece of the puzzle. Little by little, the puzzle comes together. My son would often tape the matching puzzle pieces together because of the flimsy nature of this paper puzzle. It isn't necessary, but it does give a smoother look to the final finished product. This takes almost no time to make and gives great incentives to keep moving forward in the math lesson.

The Answer Hunt

Another option is to write the answers on 3 x 5 cards, one answer per card, and then hide them in a specific room. As the child completes a problem, he gets to go hunting for the answer. When he finds it he returns to his seat with the card. On the back of each card is a word. When he has them all he can unscramble the sentence. It may be words of love from Mom. It may be a promise by Dad to play street hockey with him tonight. If you find you have more cards than words to use on the backs, just put a heart every so often as filler. Or make it a coupon good for one hug from Mom.

Time It

Some children respond well to timed games. "If you get this section done in three minutes, you'll get X, Y, Z." My son has a panic attack on timed events. But other moms with ADHD kids have used this effectively.

Limit the View

Sometimes a full page of problems is so overwhelming to these kids that they can't even begin. One way to alleviate some of shock is to dictate one problem at a time. I even write one problem per sheet of paper if the problem is a bit tedious. (I make each paper 1/4 size of a letter-sized sheet.) If he's writing it on his own rather than you writing it for him, he may have difficulty lining up the columns correctly. A method widely used in schools is to take a piece of lined writing paper and turn it sideways. This provides ready made columns.

Another trick is to cover portions of the workbook with white paper held in place by that sticky stuff used to hold up posters. Big "Post-It" notes can also be used. Kids aren't stupid. They know what's under there. But it's about focusing on one problem at a time. Somehow, just having it out of sight often eases the anxiety that a page full of math problems can elicit.

> **You don't have to do every single problem in every single section on every single page.**

If there is any lesson you should take away from this section, it should be this: *You don't have to do every single problem in every single section on every single page.* STOP! Just because there are seventeen problems on long division in today's lesson doesn't mean every child needs exactly that amount to master the concept. Some can do with much less. It certainly *feels* better to us if absolutely every item has an answer next to it. But you need to constantly ask yourself, "What am I trying to achieve here?" If your child needs to practice this concept seventeen times today, then fine. But if he mastered the concept eight lessons ago, perhaps five will suffice as a daily review. We call this "ZIP" math. I go through his lesson and circle the problems he has to do for that lesson. For about two-thirds of the lesson, he does them all. But for about one-third of the lesson, I circle just a few in each section for review. I know which ones he's mastered, so I'm comfortable with a shortened review. And he thinks he's being given a "break" because he doesn't have to do them all.

Not surprisingly, computer software is a welcome addition to the workbook grind. With its fast-paced drills and variety of games, it is tailor made for an easily distracted kid.

My son would easily spend all day playing educational games on the computer if permitted. But because many of these games are so well done and often cover the same concept being worked on in the math book, we will use them in lieu of certain sections on certain days. Usually it is given as a "reward" once a week or more for other work that was done in a timely manner or with an expected level of proficiency.

Just for fun, check out the website called *Jason's Lemonade Stand*. Your child runs a lemonade stand in the land of virtual reality for thirty days. Each day he must read the weather report and determine how much lemonade he can expect to sell the next day. He makes up his batches of lemonade, calculating cost based on current sugar prices and so on, and then lets it play out the day. There may be rain and no sales. There may be an unusually hot day, resulting in great sales. But…oops, he may run out of lemonade because he didn't plan better. It's an excellent lesson in junior economics and lots of fun.

> **One of the hallmarks of these highly distractible children is a general loathing of writing.**

Writing

One of the hallmarks of these highly distractible children is a general loathing of writing. I'm talking about the process by which thoughts are translated into the physical act of writing, not their creative abilities. These kids do not lack in the thinking department. On the contrary, they are usually quite imaginative. They can spin very complex tales complete with characters of great depth and interest. But if you ask them to write these well-developed thoughts down, it comes out as "The boy had a busy day." They are often very articulate and can retell information to you in great detail. But if they write it down, it is a masterful work in brevity.

Even the task of looking at a word written elsewhere and simply copying it onto a piece of paper is difficult for them. It struck me just how hard this was when I watched my ADHD nine-year-old sitting next to his four-year-old sister. They were both copying word lists from the whiteboard. She would glance up, see the word, and then proceed to write it down without ever looking back. She retained an image of the word in her head. My son, however, would look up, find the word, look back at his paper, write one letter, maybe two, and then he would need to look back up at the board. Even more amazingly, it took him time to find where he left off on the board. He had to totally reorient himself every time he looked away. That's when I realized that writing is truly difficult for him, and it is difficult because he is wired differently.

I also saw this problem hindering his efforts at completing his math. He knew the concept inside and out. He could articulate the solution to any problem presented and find three other approaches to the problem that worked as well. But when he went to write his answers, it was as though the solution so easily solved in his brain was now stuck on some neural pathway, pushing and shoving to get down to his pencil. It almost seemed that the part of his brain that forms thoughts could not communicate with the part of his brain that puts thoughts down on paper. It was painful for me to watch. And I'm certain that it was even more painful for him to experience. Luckily, I've read that for most of these "writing haters," it all comes together in about the fourth or fifth grade. Indeed, almost on cue, in mid-fourth grade my son developed an interest in writing poetry. He was required to write a simple haiku for a badge he was working to earn. Suddenly, he exploded in creating page after page of poems. Then he rewrote some of them so that his cursive would be as beautiful as his words. After years of his belief that any writing assignment was a punishment akin to the use of thumbscrews, this was a miracle in progress. We are not yet at the stage where he has a well-developed skill in writing or a love of the written word, but we've clearly crossed a significant line in the writing process. I'm very glad that I didn't push him during the years that he was (I believe) physically unable to make an easy connection between thought and the written word. Now that he is better able, his obvious love of communication will certainly find an outlet in the written form of expression.

If your child still struggles in crossing from thought to written word, consider allowing an oral response or a response provided by a manipulative.

If your child still struggles in crossing from thought to written word, consider allowing an oral response or a response provided by a manipulative. (See the section of this book on manipulatives for lots of ideas.) Unless you are doing an actual writing assignment, the writing may be unnecessary. Keep in mind that the object is to learn the material…not to practice writing. Writing does not necessarily have to be incorporated into every learning activity.

There are days when I will insist he plod through it and write down each answer. After all, I do want these two portions of the brain to eventually learn to talk to each other quickly and fluidly. But there are days when the goal of the lesson—let's say math—is being lost in my efforts to have him connect math and writing. Don't hesitate to isolate the concept being studied if that's what works for your child. If you are not willing to do this, you may find yourself in an unfortunate situation where your child is falling behind in a subject, in which he is perfectly capable, because you insist he do it in tandem with a subject he isn't yet capable of handling with ease.

I have a final thought on writing as it pertains to handwriting, as in neatness, spacing, general legibility, etc. I know of people who place great emphasis on the importance of beautiful penmanship. Indeed, at one point in history it was the mark of a true gentleman.

I, too, see it as a value. But I don't believe for an instant that my child will never find direction in life if he can't master a beautiful script. I say this for several reasons. First, my husband has had a good measure of success in his life, both academically and professionally, and yet his handwriting is deplorable. (I'll save his spelling for another time!) In fact, I've never seen worse. Compared to his, the handwriting of most doctors is a work of art. And that brings me to the second reason. Everyone knows that doctors are notorious for horrible penmanship. No one would argue that poor writing has limited their success in life! And last of all, we're are pretty entrenched into the computer age. And good keyboarding skills will cover a multitude of penmanship sins. (Not to mention the sins of spelling and grammar.) So while we do indeed have penmanship as a part of our schooling efforts, I don't hang my son's future on his mastery of this skill or lack thereof.

History

History is the perfect subject for our special kids because it lends itself so readily to the concept of "Being the Lesson." It is not only easy, but fun to act out the period of history being studied. It's so easy to make a salt dough map of the geographic region, to sew period clothes, duplicate period food, or sketch period housing. We love history in our house. And this is most definitely *not* due to a prior love of history throughout my own education. Aren't you glad it's never too late to have a good education?

There are many approaches to teaching history. I don't know about you, but my educational career had me and most of my fellow students believing that the world began when Columbus discovered America. We spent year after year hearing the basic story of America over and over again. Oh, we heard about pyramids once in a while. But by and large, it seemed that most of history occurred in the last 300 years. Then, suddenly in high school, all the previous thousands of years were crammed into an eighteen week study. I could certainly tell you who was our first president, but by the end of the year, I wasn't sure if Cleopatra was an Egyptian, a Viking, or the cousin of King Arthur. This disjointed presentation of history seems almost unnatural. And it certainly will *not* aid the spirited child, whose thinking is already disjointed by his constant distractedness, to develop a framework upon which to hang pieces of historical information he comes upon as he continues learning.

Our preferred approach is to teach the child history in the chronological order in which it occurred. We also like to spend a substantial amount of time on each section, living and breathing that period of history for a year. We started with the beginning, and did a thorough study of Genesis. Then we hit ancient Egypt, ancient Greece, ancient Rome, and so on through time. The child learns about history as it unfolded. One curriculum that does this extremely well is published by Greenleaf Press. They do not spend years on American history only to have world history crammed into a few short months near the end of a child's academic training. The emphasis is not on dates, but on events and the interesting lives of people. (Dates can always be obtained if you remember the event or person you're looking for.) Furthermore, they are dedicated to providing materials that are void of dull, lifeless information.

While we use Greenleaf materials, which are an excellent resource, it is still essential to supplement with lots of hands-on activities as well as period autobiographies and books of historical fiction that take your child back into the time period you are studying. I must also admit that I have borrowed an idea from Kelly, a fellow homeschooler in my support group. Whenever Thanksgiving rolls around, we leave the time period we've been studying and make a brief journey into the more recent American history. Such a major celebration requires some background information. And when we eventually hit that time period in full force, our kids will already be familiar with some names and events.

Last of all, it is worthwhile to purchase or make a good time line. Children will be so absorbed by their own American history that it will seem equal in time to many other periods. It is amazing to them to realize how young America is compared to some ancient civilizations.

There are other studies of history that have similar approaches. *Beautiful Feet* is one that divides sections of history into unit studies. So these, too, could be done in order. Whatever approach to history you are using, make it come alive with plenty of supplemental activity that involves making and doing.

Pulling It All Together in Your Plan Book

Knowing all sorts of ways to make a lesson interesting is different than actually doing it day in and day out. As your child gets older, he will become more tolerant of learning that is not fun and interesting. While that says something good about his development, it is a poor excuse for slipping into a dull, regimented learning day. To ward against a monotonous routine, I've developed a color code for my plan book. If I place a green "M" over an item, it means we've used a manipulative of some sort. A blue star signifies the use of a game. An orange "V" shows the viewing of a video. A purple star indicates a field trip. And a pink "AP" means that we've done an art project. When I look over my week's plans, I expect to see color all over the place. If I don't, then I change my plans.

Chapter 8

I Can't Take Him Anywhere!

Field Trips

One of the educational benefits that most homeschooling support groups offer is a great variety of field trips. Early in our homeschooling efforts, I attended as many as possible to duplicate the school experience I felt I was withholding from my child. That dreaded "need for socialization" dragged us to many a field trip. (The whole issue regarding the concern over socialization has been eloquently and very humorously addressed in a book by Rick Boyer, called *The Socialization Trap*. I highly recommend this book to homeschoolers early in their homeschooling careers.)

While field trips, in and of themselves, are not a problem, groups of children have a frenzying effect on our special children. Jennifer, another homeschooling mom of a highly spirited child, shared with me that her son seems to gobble up the random energy in the group, and then it becomes multiplied in his own system. In a large group, much of your time will simply be spent trying to keep visual contact with your child as he darts about. There is practically no meaningful conversation. You will also probably spend a good portion of time keeping him from crossing "that line" that high energy kids can easily cross under such circumstances. Over time I have realized that it is much better for my son (and for me) if we go on the trip alone, or maybe with one other family. Now, instead of constantly trying to help him rein in the frenzy on Zoo Day, we can have thoughtful conversation about animal habits, diets, social order, and the amazing detail and intricacies of God's creation. The day ends with an increased understanding of the subject matter and a memory of good times spent with family instead of exhaustion born of frustration and constant reprimands.

Sitting Still in Church

There are a few anointed saints who firmly believe that a child should be sitting in the pew with their parents from age six weeks. A greater majority think it dreadful if your child is not in the pew with you from at least age three forward. But in our house, it was not even possible to contemplate that until well after the age of five. And even then it was a struggle.

People who have never personally been around a truly hyperactive child will watch your child and assume they are observing a major lack of discipline.

People who have never personally been around a truly hyperactive child will watch your child and assume they are observing a major lack of discipline. This said, please be kind in your judgment of these uninformed folks. I must admit that if my daughter were my only child, I, too, would hold the same interpretation of hyperactive behavior. In fact, if all my children behaved as did my daughter, I would most likely be quite arrogant about my superior parenting skills. I have met such folks, and they would never dream that genetics played any part in the calm, compliant ways of their children. So while you and I know better, be gracious in this knowledge.

I've always assumed that others in church were horribly annoyed by my son's behavior. Even if they were not distracted by his constant movement or his seeming inability to whisper, I was. Worship was one of the few moments in my week where I needed to be focused on something other than my child. Instead of the uplifting and recentering event that it should be, it was stressful and defeating for both of us. And it often meant that my husband or I had to leave with our son, deal with the discipline issue, and spend the remainder of the service straining to feel a part of worship from the foyer. We had to find other options.

For a time, we attended no Sunday School ourselves but went to church while our son was in Sunday School. Eventually, we chose to have our son attend two Sunday School classes back-to-back rather than bring him into the sanctuary to worship with us. This is not possible in many churches, as they have Sunday School for only one hour. I know of some families who are in the unfortunate position of trading off between the parents, so that only one can attend the worship service per week. You will eventually be able to take him into worship. We began taking him with us at age five, but it was at least two years before we could count on an uneventful service. Things greatly improved when he became a solid reader. I had many more options for busy work that kept the wiggles at bay.

An activity that holds my son's attention for a long period of time is solving a "Bible Verse in Code." I simply take a Bible verse, assign some odd shape to each letter (circle, circle with a dot in it, circle with a line through it, etc.), and rewrite the verse in code. To get him started, I usually give him the answer code for the letters "e" and "t." Not only is he getting exposure to Bible verses, but he is developing good critical thinking skills as well.

Just to add an element of real anticipation, I've included a hundred-point bonus word. It is always a highly unlikely word, such as coffee, laboratory, spaceship.

Another activity that he really seems to enjoy we call "Sermon Points." I've made a piece of paper containing words that he is likely to hear in the sermon. He checks them off as he hears them. He gets one point for the really common ones (Jesus, God, Lord). He gets five points for less frequent words (save/saved, forgive, believe, worship, power). Ten points for tougher finds. (blood, obey, listen, glory/glorify). Thirty points for some real finds (righteous/righteousness, evil, faith, heaven, kingdom). And just to add an element of real anticipation, I've included a hundred-point bonus word. It is always a highly unlikely word, such as coffee, laboratory, spaceship. The game begins only when the pastor starts the sermon. Music and announcements don't count. To play this game my son has to actually pay attention to the sermon. If he accumulates 200 points or more, he wins the game. The reward for us is that we go out for lunch after church, and he can choose the place. Just select the reward that will best motivate your child.

I feared that too much of "Sermon Points" would encourage a sort of "auditory scanning." I played the game a few times myself and discovered I could hear the words coming out of the pastor's mouth without really hearing them in context. In other words, I could play the game without really listening. Because of this concern, I was greatly interested when I heard of a drawing activity done in church by a good friend of mine. It turns the sermons into "Sermon Pictures." A regular-sized piece of copying paper or typing paper is divided into eight equal sections. As the pastor preaches, you visualize some picture that would encapsulate the concept he is speaking on first. What practical lesson is the most memorable part of the sermon? What do you need to take away from this sermon and put into practice? Keep the figures simple. Stick drawings are the norm. Add a few words if necessary to explain the picture. You will never be accused of auditory scanning with this

"Finding time for God"

activity. You simply cannot do this without listening to the sermon, internalizing the message, and reproducing it in visual form.

What has amazed me is is how much I retain about the sermons, even months later. With a mere glance at my page, I can recount much of the sermon to you. If you have a highly visual child, he may take to this immediately. While my children are still reluctant to do the drawing, they still show an interest in what I am drawing. I have continued to do this, not only for my own sake, but because it makes so very clear to my children what is being said.

We've also found several great games grouped together in a sort of booklet pad entitled *Church Worship Pages* available from Sycamore Tree. There are twelve reproducible pages of games and activities directed at children ages 6 - 13 to be used during a worship service. One of my favorites is much like a game we've all played in the car. Look for a word (or in this case, listen) that starts with an "A." After that, find a word that starts with "B," then "C," and so on through the alphabet. They have a nice page with connected circles that takes your child through the whole alphabet. There is also a game similar to Bingo, based again upon the pastor's words, and many more.

> **What has amazed me is is how much I retain about the sermons, even months later. With a mere glance at my page, I can recount much of the sermon to you.**

Let Him Know What's Coming

Kids that are hard-wired on to a faster track do not like big surprises. This is especially true with ADHD kids. Any major change in what they expect to happen in their day is a negative event. They like to know what is coming and when. They seem to sort of prewire themselves for expectations of the day or of an event. A major deviation from their expectations can send them reeling. They feel very out of control when things are happening that were not part of their prewiring. That is why, whenever possible, it is important to tell your child what to expect...even if it is an event that would never require any previous information for you. "When we go to Aunt Tilly's today, let me tell you what kinds of things are probably going to happen." Tell him which uncle may get a little boisterous, which wall has Aunt Tilly's beloved but breakable teacup collection, and what the smells, sights, and sounds will be. Also make clear ahead of time what your expectations are for his behavior. Never assume he has any prior knowledge of what is acceptable. It should be clearly explained that his recent attempts at burping in Morse code are not appropriate at Aunt Tilly's, even if Uncle Frank engages in something similar.

In the same way, school should be generally what he expects it to be. My son clearly feels more a part of the process when I give him a list of the items we will be covering that day. He looks over the list and does a sort of wiring for the day's events. He feels less like he is "at my mercy to meander wherever I choose" and more a part of a thought-out plan. It also seems to be immensely satisfying to him to be able to check off a completed item. He has even gotten to the point now that he makes checklists for himself when he has a multitiered task to accomplish.

Peace in the Car

I remember how much I enjoyed the time spent in the car with my son when he was very young. We were "road buddies" having great conversations, singing silly songs, and sharing ridiculous jokes. When I had a second child I thought, "How wonderful! Now we'll have an addition to our fun-filled road buddies club." I think Webster's dictionary has now changed the definition of "naive" to "Go ask Carol about more than one kid in a car." Or perhaps you could just look up the word "horrendous." There is nothing worse than the "she-touched-me-no-I-didn't-I-breathed-on-you-because-you-looked-out-my-window-blah-blah-blah" routine. You know by now that many of the previously mentioned materials can be taken in the car. But that requires that while you were making the mad dash to the car, running back to get one more coat, and seeing to it that everyone hit the bathroom first, you also were organized enough to plan and bring learning materials along for each child to occupy them for the duration of the trip. Not surprisingly, there are many trips where I find myself in a car with two squabbling kids and no creative material to engage them.

Not surprisingly, there are many trips where I find myself in a car with two squabbling kids and no creative material to engage them.

These two ideas are not earth-shatteringly creative, but they have made a significant difference in the peace in our car rides. The first is obvious. Cassette tapes. I'm sure that many of you use cassette tapes in the car. They truly are magical in their ability to bring silence. I've discovered they're much more useful if they are stories rather than just songs. One series we have played to death is the Classical Kids series about famous musical composers. These are exciting, stimulating stories seen from the eyes of a child living in the time and place of a well-known composer. *Vivaldi's Ring of Mystery* is probably our favorite. Putting this tape on brings instant silence to my car. Also in the series is *Mozart's Magic Fantasy*, *Beethoven Lives Upstairs*, *Mr. Bach Comes to Call*, *Hallelujah Handel*, and *Tchaikovsky Comes to America*. The incredible side benefit to these tapes is your child's exposure to and recognition of great works of music. Many is the time that my four-year-old would hear a piece of music on a TV commercial or in a waiting room and be delighted that she recognized it as Tchaikovsky. My son, who does not possess a natural music ability, would say, "That doesn't sound exactly like Vivaldi, but it's similar. I wonder if it's from the same period." I could read to my children for weeks and play excerpts of music till I'm blue in the face, and I would still not impart as much learning and love of music to my children as has been accomplished by these tapes.

Another inexpensive option is to borrow tapes from the library. Most libraries have lots of stand-alone cassettes. We prefer their book-tape combinations because of our preference for stories over sing-a-longs. After losing one of the library's tapes, I made my own by recording myself reading some of my children's favorite stories. This is an inexpensive option, albeit a bit time-consuming one. You could always have one child read aloud in the car to all the others, but always watch for telltale signs of motion sickness.

Here is yet another idea borrowed from a homeschooling mom. She has subscriptions to several science magazines. The children certainly think the magazines are interesting. But when the latest copies are at home, sometimes they are picked up and read, sometimes they are not. There are many things at home that can distract a child away from reading. So this mom decided to keep them in her car. Now you have a captive and bored audience. They will read anything. I tried this with instant success. I usually pick up these magazines for ten cents at garage sales or at library sales. I keep about ten of them at a time in my car in a plastic box that rests between my two children. When they have read them from cover to cover several times, I rotate them.

Chapter 9

What About Spanking?

Discipline is a major component of parenting, but with highly stimulated children, it takes on special dimensions. These children often respond very differently than other children to the exact same events. This is probably more true in the arena of discipline than in any other. Like all parents of just such a child, we have struggled to find the best discipline methods for our child. And certainly, discipline (the variety that is most often externally applied) is the first thing that parents of typical children will offer as a solution. "What that boy needs is a good…!" You can fill in the blank, I'm sure. We've run the gamut of discipline philosophies and programs in our home. Let me make very clear that I am not anti-spanking. But I can also tell you from experience that when we attempted to utilize one of the more heavily spanking-incorporated philosophies in our household it was a horrible experience for the entire family. I am almost certain there are those who use this philosophy in a godly and loving way and it provides peace and stability in their home. And I am also almost certain they would probably say that we had done it incorrectly. And they may be right. But I know that what I was doing did not feel loving or Godly. After a time, I felt very strongly that I was losing my son. So we abandoned this approach.

I feel compelled to tell you that spanking was a part of my own upbringing and caused no distancing between me and my parents. When I was spanked, I knew it was justice at work. I had done wrong. It was clear to me that I had done wrong. It had been within my power to do right, and I had not done it. But the key words here are "within my power." It is so much more difficult with an ADHD child to determine just which behaviors are willful disobedience and which ones cross over into his very real problem area of "impulse control." By no means am I saying that it is impossible for these children to direct their own behavior. Indeed, one of the main purposes of our choice to homeschool is to accomplish discipline and self-control. But the very same behavior that can be easily avoided by a typical child may be much more difficult for the spirited child to avoid, particularly in a state of excitement—a state, by the way, sometimes caused by our own parenting style or by a situation in which we place the child. If I take little Jacob to one of those indoor kids' playgrounds with all the accompanying squeals, screams, buzzes, and sirens, I certainly have no right to be shocked when Jacob loses control and steps over the line. In other words, an action may reflect extreme willful disobedience if Billy does it, but it may be only barely willful if Jacob does it. While children certainly must learn that consequences follow their actions, punishments and discipline directed at building character and responsibility should reflect that willfulness and intent.

> **It is so much more difficult with an ADHD child to determine just which behaviors are willful disobedience and which ones cross over into his very real problem area of "impulse control."**

It took me a while to realize that my son could not regulate his behavior in exactly the same way that most of the rest of us can. Years ago, there was an instance when my son became extraordinarily distraught because he wanted me to *turn back time* so that he could replay an event and achieve a different outcome. (Yes, he may have been exposed to *Star Trek* at far too young an age.) I was still at the stage where I believed I could reason with him. But the more I explained the impossibility of his request, the worse he became. He wasn't just unhappy. He became so distraught that he reminded me of some of the autistic children I used to work with. He was gesticulating in a rhythmical fashion, tensing and relaxing his muscles, making sounds and wailing all at the same time. And it escalated from there. I finally realized that he was so out of control that even *he* couldn't get it back. It was no longer within his power. And by continuing on the same path of trying to reason with him, I was only making it worse, not only for me but for him. It was as though he had crossed a line from which he could not return on his own. It was painful to watch. And it must have been frightening for him to be so driven by internal forces he didn't understand

74

and over which he seemingly had no control. I have learned since how important it is to keep him from ever crossing that line again. I keep a tighter rein on the direction of our disagreements. With time I have discovered how to recognize early that we are on a path that could get out of hand. If I quickly get him to move on to some other task or thought and then give him a bit of space, he usually can reorient himself to a self-controlled state on his own.

Any discipline method that you choose must include a wise reading of the facts and an effort to dispense true justice. It is very easy with our intense, highly stimulated children to find yourself dealing with some punishment at almost every turn. So you must ask yourself, "What was the intent?"

Accomplishing this goal is not as hard as it sounds. We apply such standards every day. For example, imagine I am walking down the aisle of a crowded bus. A kid stands up quickly without looking and inadvertently bumps me, rather hard in fact, but then he apologizes profusely. My arm is slightly sore, but I am not angry. It was not intentional. But if on the same bus another kid starts from the back, running and pushing people out of his way to get to the front. When he gets to me I move just in time to avoid being roughly shoved aside. In the latter case he did not actually touch me. In fact, he caused me no true harm. Yet I would find myself angry because I am fully aware of his intention. If I were dispensing justice, I would apply grace to the first kid who actually did cause harm, and I would apply something else to the second.

> **Any discipline method that you choose must include a wise reading of the facts and an effort to dispense true justice.**

Impulse control is a very real issue for these kids. I have seen my son make an unwise decision and then show immediate remorse. When I have asked him why he made this choice, with tears in his eyes and confusion in his voice he cries, "I just don't know!" Because their brains are churning out ideas at warp speed, the mechanism the rest of us use to pause and reflect on the wisdom of each idea is just not able to keep up in this child's mind. The results? More injuries during their childhood. They have no fear. They'll climb on that weak branch. They'll leap from the top of the bunk bed. They'll enthusiastically roll around on the floor until their head makes contact with a solid piece of furniture. Another result we must guard closely against is that these rapidly acted upon thoughts can often lead to an injury of a playmate or sibling. For obvious reasons, this impulsive behavior can make it difficult for the child to maintain friendships…and can even distance the whole family from other families.

The way we have handled this issue has been to keep our son in groups that are small and are within our view. He can play with one or two neighborhood boys, but if more show up, he must politely excuse himself and return home. When we go to a friend's house, I am always within view or earshot of him. This way I am usually able to tell just by the sound that the level of intensity is reaching a point where a bad decision is likely to occur. One or two choice words can redirect the moment onto a safer path. As he has gotten older and more able to control his impulses, I have lengthened the reins a bit. But any evidence of poor judgment causes a retightening of the reins. This method is best used when accompanied by an explanation that it is not a punishment, but rather another tool to help him strengthen his own ability to judge his actions before acting on them. And since he is very sincere in his desire to *not* hurt his friends, he understands and accepts this advice. (Well…most of the time.)

Any stimulus is magnified for the intensely spirited child. It's as though everything that enters through his ear is set on "loud" and cannot be turned down.

Any stimulus is magnified for the intensely spirited child. It's as though everything that enters through his ear is set on "loud" and cannot be turned down. And what's more, our natural ability to screen out sounds and sights that are not relevant to our task is an ability that is immature in these children. He will take in all stimuli and give them all equal weight. Every response he gives is likewise magnified. If his sister bumps him accidently, a minor rebuke would be appropriate. But often instead we get an explosive, "Katie! Look what you made me do! You are so careless! You should have to clean my room for a year!" In the past, my response used to reflect my belief that he was just being mean-spirited and that punishment was in order. But now I've come to the conclusion that he truly doesn't understand what an appropriate response is. You may be thinking, "Why can't he just watch you, the parent, and learn through modeling just what an appropriate response looks like?" The problem is in perceptions. He watches us respond mildly to a mild stimulus. And he also watches us respond stronger to a stronger stimulus. But because things are magnified in his head, he *never has a mild stimulus*! So he feels fully justified in producing a major response to almost every infraction, because to him, they are all major.

We have begun a response training program to deal with the overreactions that are typical. First, we rate the response. "On a scale of 1-10, was that nine? Maybe even a ten?" Then, I explain that five would have been more appropriate. I have him reword his response, change his tone, and try it again. We may even role-play it a few times. The final act in this exercise is that he still needs to apologize for the initial outburst. This is a much more useful response. It is information he can actually use to modify his behavior. Amazingly, there have even been a few times lately when he produces a major response, pauses a moment, and then says, "Sorry, I know that was too strong." Now that's a life skill.

All that said regarding stimuli and overreacting, let's return to the subject of spanking. Well, spanking is a *big* stimulus and is no different. It too is greatly magnified inside this child. What seems to be a simple spanking to you is a highly multiplied shock wave for this already intensified child. While I believe this to be the case, to be honest, I'm not certain just what to do with the information. I do think we were right to work with other methods of discipline in our house. For what it's worth, we have had the most success with a program found in a book called *1-2-3 Magic* by Thomas Phelan. I don't agree with everything in the book (for example, if your child wants to throw a fit and trash his room, let him. He'll only have to clean it up later). Additionally, we want some time spent on sin—the cause of bad behavior, repentance, and forgiveness. Nonetheless, the basics of the program have worked well for us. Whatever discipline method that you choose must include a wise reading of the facts and an effort to dispense true justice. Regardless of the system or approach or method you use, I believe that a child who is secure in his parents' love, who feels appreciated for the uniqueness of his makeup, who is often reminded that God has special plans for all this energy, all coupled together with time, will result in a child who does learn how to behave and be respectful.

Chapter 10

See the Gift in This Child

You will undoubtedly come in contact with others who do not see your child as a "gift." I know that many other moms watch with horror as I calmly extract my child from the top of the refrigerator upon which he has climbed. They grow weary as he shares with me the three millionth thought that has just flashed into his head. They even comment that they could never handle a child with the energy level of my son, while I harbor the belief that they also think I should just make him "straighten up!" Many, I'm certain, believe a lack of discipline is at the root of his behavior.

Others have commented that I seem to hold the reins of discipline too tightly. I recall when a friend of mine said that a parent's response to a child's behavior can run from 1-10. In her opinion, I seemed to always head straight to 10. I do indeed keep a "shorter leash" with this child, for I know that there is a line of excitement where, once crossed, he will act on any impulse immediately, without concern for consequences or dangers to himself or others. So to these parents of calm, compliant children, I *do* seem to respond too quickly to what appears to be a very minor infraction. But I know what comes later if things aren't kept in check now.

So I have learned to smile politely when their well-meaning comments are sometimes way off base. I know a secret. While all children are gifts, this child is extra special. I really believe that my son is destined for something wonderful—something that would be impossible for those calmer, regular-energy level children. I can think of several occupations where boundless energy would be an incredible asset. I delight in the fast pace of his thought. I smile at his intense indignation at one of the world's many injustices. I am even jealous of his tireless enthusiasm for life and wonder what more I could accomplish if I were so blessed. And I am most especially delighted that I have been chosen to help him rein in and shape this gift of boundless energy.

If my son were in a traditional school setting, he most certainly would have been labeled a "troublemaker," and he probably would have believed it himself.

In an effort to keep *your* energy up, be careful of the amount of time you spend in the company of those who view your child or your decisions for this child negatively. I know these folks cannot always be avoided. But raising a highly spirited child requires much energy to maintain a positive attitude. Find a group of people who understand your child and schedule time in your lives to be around them.

On days when you wonder if you and homeschooling are your child's best option, keep in mind that the very best public school teacher in the very best school system with the very best of awareness and the very best of intentions still cannot keep this child from getting into trouble in a room with twenty-five other children. If my son were in a traditional school setting, he most certainly would have been labeled a "troublemaker," and he probably would have believed it himself. At home we have the opportunity to take the world's view of this child and flip it. The world sees him as one who will most likely always be in trouble due to a defect beyond his control. We can exchange this view for one in which this child has been fortunate enough to receive a supercharged gift of energy that only needs to be harnessed, fine-tuned, and properly directed so that he can take on the world as others cannot. You can teach him to be cautious with the power in this gift. You can teach him to be grateful for the opportunities in this gift. And you can teach him that God expects much out of him as a result of this gift.

Not only must you see your child's qualities as a gift for *him*, but you need to see the gift that God has given *you* when He chose you as the parent of such a child. What is it that God wishes for you in this arrangement? If you let go and accept God's wisdom in designing your child this way, you will find yourself challenged to grow in ways that can only benefit you and your walk with Him. You will develop patience. You'll see life from a bigger perspective and get "ruffled" less easily by its inevitable ups and downs. You'll be less harsh in your judgment of others and better able to step in and provide comfort to those in need. Your empathy will come from heartfelt experience. You'll possess a calmness during stress. Indeed, you will come to view stress differently than before. You will develop a joy at God's amazing provision, as you will have called upon Him countless times only to find Him ready and able to supply your need. And when your walk is strengthened, it has a rippling effect over the walks of all your children.

After years of wondering what God was thinking when He filled my child with such qualities, I finally let go, trusted the Designer, and began to explore them. Had I sent my child off to public school, I am certain that he never would have perceived these qualities as anything nearing a gift. I am so very thankful that my son's image of himself is of a creative, innovative, intelligent, can-do child. I am thankful that he has an ego that more often needs to be reined in rather than pieced together in weak fragments. I am thankful that his image of himself and his faith are not under daily attack. I am truly thankful for his ADHD, for in it I see the gift in this child, both for him and for me. I pray that you too will explore this gift given to you and your family and begin to find the Designer's plan for your child.

Reproducible Resources for Home and Classroom Use

1. Corn Root Aphid

2. Spanish body parts

3. Boo Boo Bear

4. Deliver the Mail

5. Rainbow

6. Bingo Blanks

7. Beetle Bingo

8. Bear Belly Bingo

9. Sample Cards for Bear Belly Bingo

10. Vicky Velpanoid from Venus

11. Milnerd Moonman

12. Roadblock

13. Math workbook puzzle

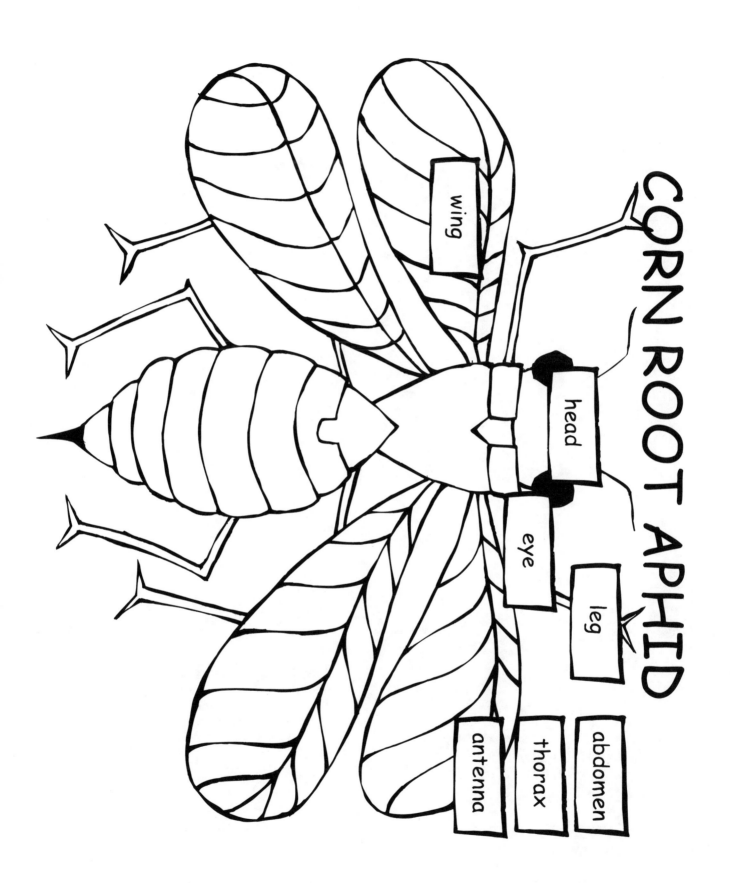

CORN ROOT APHID

wing

head

eye

leg

antenna

thorax

abdomen

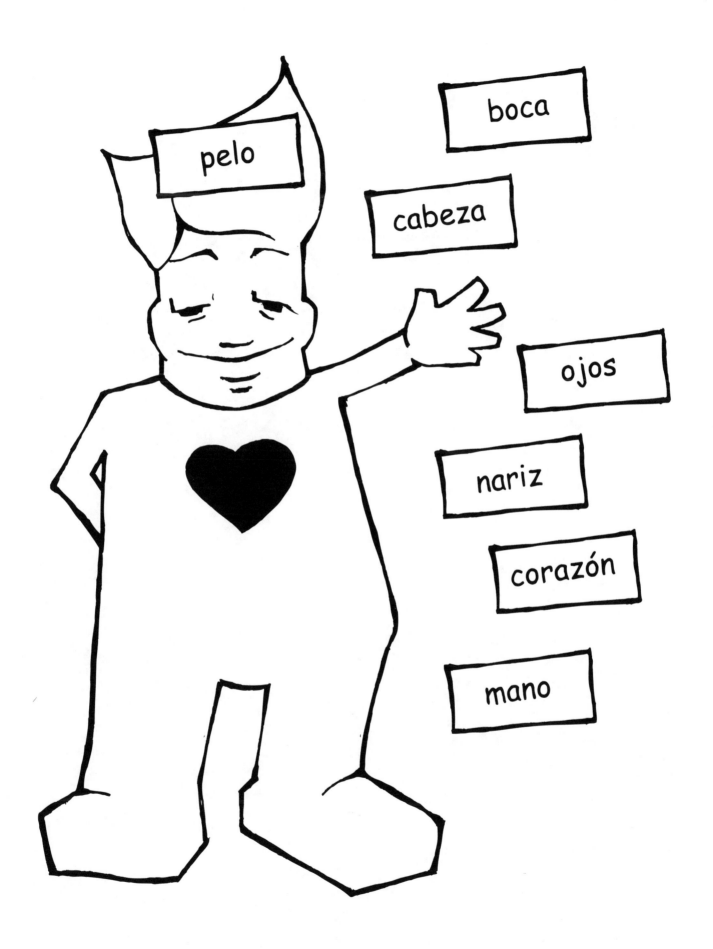

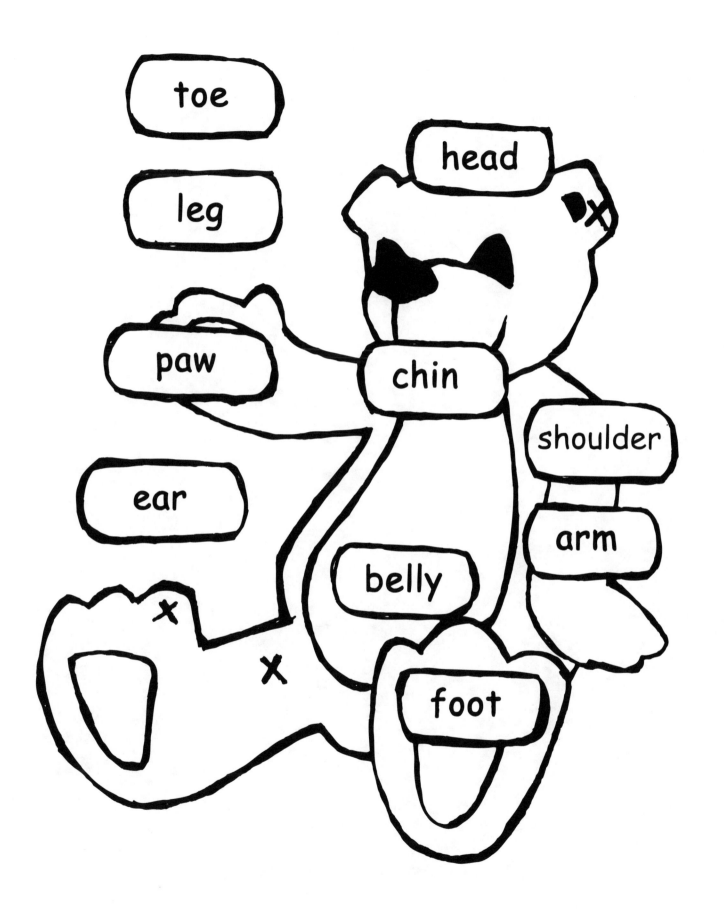

Deliver Mail

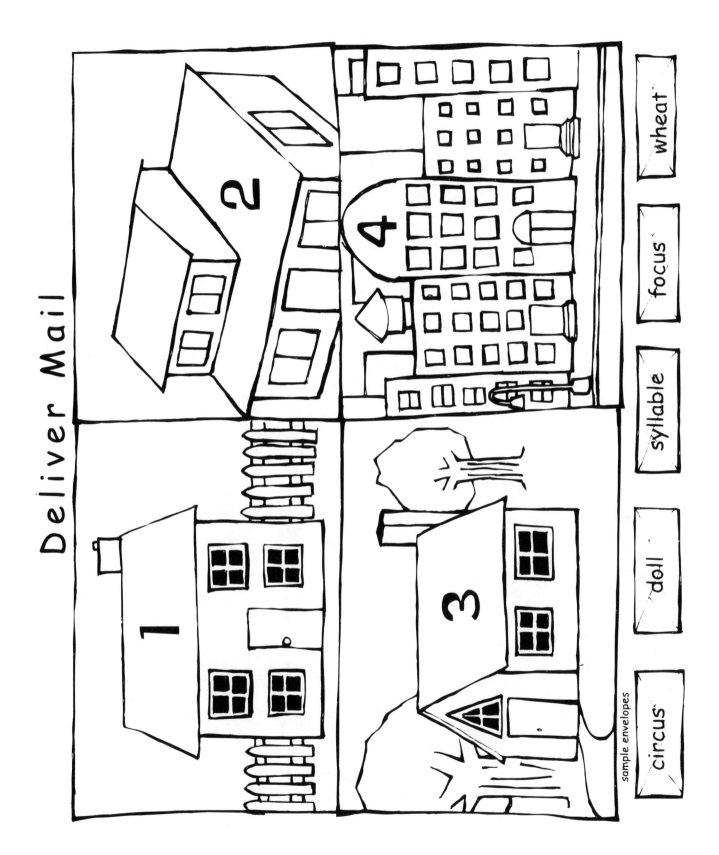

1

2

4

3

sample envelopes

circus   doll   syllable   focus   wheat

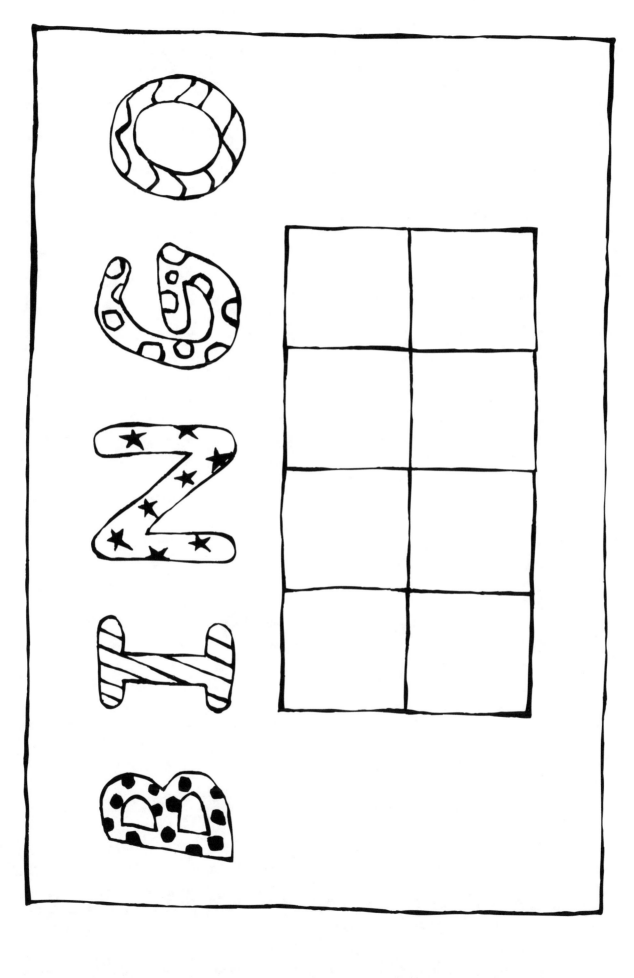

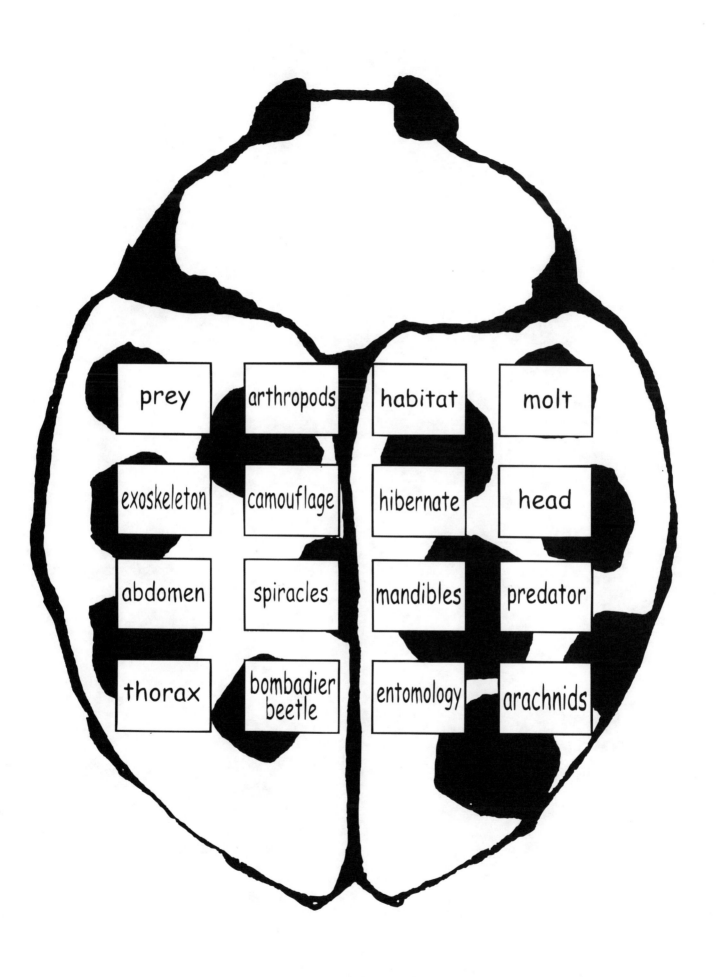

Sample Cards
to use with
Bear Belly Bingo

Vicky Velpanoid from Venus

Milnerd Moonman

FUEL

YOU'RE #ONE!!!

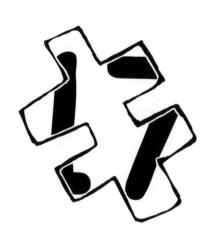

Use in sections to turn math workbooks into puzzles.

Resource List

1-2-3 Magic
Thomas W. Phelan, Ph.D.
Child Management Inc., 1995
(Can be ordered at 1-800-442-4453)

Beautiful Feet
www.bfbooks.com
(Catalog can be ordered at 508-833-8626)

Calc-U-Draw
Buki Toys, Buki Ltd.

Church Worship Pages
Sandra Gogel
The Sycamore Tree
(Catalog available at 949-650-4466)

Games for Learning
Peggy Kaye

Games for Math
The Noonday Press, 1991

Games for Reading
Often found in local libraries and bookstores

Games for Writing

Greenleaf History Materials
Greenleaf Press
(Catalog can be ordered at 615-449-1617)

Jason's Lemonade Stand
www.Littlejason.com/lemonade/

The Socialization Trap
Rick Boyer

Games—Tools for Learning
Janice and Mark Vreeland
(Order at 414-327-4228)

Fun Thinkers Books
Educational Insights

Fun Thinkers Match Frames

Plyhedra Dice Games
Don Balka
Ideal School Supply Company
(Catalog can be ordered at 1-800-845-8149)

The Classic Kids Collection

Vivaldi's Ring of Mystery	*Beethoven Lives Upstairs*
Mr. Bach Comes to Call	*Mozart's Magic Fantasy*
Hallelujah Handel	*Mozart's Magnificent Voyage*
Tchaikovsky Discovers America	